Charnwood

Charnwood is the name of a very remarkable nursery centre which gives handicapped and normal children the opportunity to play, learn and grow up together, and provides much-needed support for parents. Today the experts readily acknowledge the all-round benefits, to both normal and handicapped children, of this kind of integrated education. In the 1960s, when Grace Wyatt's pioneer work began, it was frowned on and even considered harmful—and there were many battles to fight before the Charnwood centre earned the recognition it so obviously deserved.

This is a story, especially, of handicapped children and their families, the agonies and the triumphs. It carries a strong message of hope for all who are in any way involved with handicap, and for the 'normal' too—a way through the initial embarrassment so many feel, to real relationship. There is joy in loving a child purely for who he or she is, and great reward in seeing children with different abilities play together in a child-world untouched by labels and restrictions.

To Felicity, who inspired our endeavours,
and to John, whose vision and constant
support made them possible

Charnwood

GRACE WYATT WITH CLIVE LANGMEAD

A LION PAPERBACK
Tring · Batavia · Sydney

Copyright © 1987 Grace Wyatt and Clive Langmead

Published by
Lion Publishing plc
Icknield Way, Tring, Herts, England
ISBN 0 7459 1137 4
Albatross Books Pty Ltd
PO Box 320, Sutherland, NSW 2232, Australia
ISBN 0 86760 870 6

First edition 1987
Reprinted 1987

British Library Cataloguing in Publication Data
Wyatt, Grace
  Charnwood.
  1. Charnwood (*play group*)
  I. Title II. Langmead, Clive
  372'.216 LB1140.25.G7
  ISBN 0-7459-1137-4

Printed and bound in Great Britain
by Cox and Wyman Ltd, Reading

CONTENTS

AUTHOR'S NOTE

I have found it very hard to retell the story of Charnwood. Not only because of reawakened emotions or sensitivity to traumatic events, though both these are deeply true. Reliving the pleasures and pains of the past is notoriously arduous, especially when each experience has to be carefully selected, picked over and analysed again and again to ensure accuracy and fairness. No one appears without permission, and in places names have been changed to protect the privacy of individuals. I hope I have achieved this.

The biggest difficulty I have faced is in the omissions I have been forced to make—largely through the constraint of telling the story in one brief volume. If I had had my way, the Charnwood story would have run to as many volumes as *The Encyclopedia Britannica*! So many faces and friends have been left out: so many people I would have dearly loved to mention. Some of the closest supporters of our work have not even been mentioned in passing. Many, many of the children, and their mothers, who have passed through Charnwood—some of whose trials and triumphs still ring loudly in my memory—have been excluded.

I must, however, acknowledge here a special debt

of gratitude to my colleagues at Charnwood for contributions made so generously to all aspects of its development, and to members of the Preschool Playgroup Association who have greatly influenced my thinking and practice. I am deeply grateful for the friendship of special mothers—too many to identify—who have given so much; for the support of many secretaries—Diane, Muriel, Kathy, Jane, Gill and Janice—and for the unlimited courage and patience of the Trustees of Charnwood.

It is impossible satisfactorily to compress thirty years of work, moment by moment, into just a few pages. All I can offer are the simple contours of the landscape in the hope that those who choose to view it can gain, through drawing on their own experiences of life, some idea of the detail.

That certainly is my prayer—and also that all who read, and hopefully enjoy this book, will be able to see the hand that drew in the contours in the first place.

Grace Wyatt
'Charnwood'
Stockport 1986

For readers who would like to contact the Centre, the address is: 'Charnwood', St Paul's Road, Heaton Moor, Stockport SK4 4RY

Chapter One

FELICITY

I had expected to feel happier about it all. I really
had. After all, I was a professional nursery teacher
and the little girl had been brought along to the
playgroup at my invitation. But I was nervous and
uncertain. Was it another case of emotion triumph-
ing over common sense? Perhaps I had been wrong to
ask her.

I watched the little group approach the gate. A
mother and two children—two girls. One was
walking, the other was being carried.

I stood at the entrance to the Coach House—the
small 'gingerbread house' where I held my morning
playgroup. At one time it had been a real coach
house, to the rear of a dentist's surgery in Heaton
Moor, a suburb of Stockport, close to the great city of
Manchester.

Every morning the Coach House played host to a
group of forty or so pre-school children, aged from
around three to five years old. It was their morning of
discovery. They had books, toys, rides, storytime,
music time, sandpit-time, time to rush up stairs,
peep out of windows and wave at their friends, and
then rush down again. They had places where they
could sit and colour, or stand up and paint, places to

9

make adventure camps or pretend houses and kitchens, places to dress up as doctors and nurses or as mothers and fathers—with a wide selection of dolls and teddy bears to make well-behaved 'babies' too. There was laughter and, inevitably, a few tears — soon comforted by one of the many adult helpers who assisted me.

In short it was a typical playgroup: a place to run and jump and play games, a place to learn, to discover about life and what fun it could be.

But this child—this new little girl—could do none of that. Her mother carried her up the path, the summer breeze stirring her dress and the leaves of the apple tree in the garden. The air smelled wet, warning of a shower to come. I felt tears of pity in my heart. For Felicity was severely handicapped—something entirely outside my experience.

I had known about her, and her condition, for some time. She was the sister of one of the little girls already in the playgroup. As a consequence I had followed the story at a distance.

Shortly after birth Felicity had been diagnosed as having muscular atrophy—a condition which affected the muscles throughout her body, causing many of them to be weak and wasted. As so often happens with handicapped children the doctors saw little hope or potential for her—and told her parents so, but whenever I saw her at the Coach House I noticed her bright interest in everything that happened.

'She looks a bright little button to me!' I exclaimed one day, when her parents were dropping off her sister and seemed particularly despondent about the future. 'I'm sure we'll be able to manage her in the playgroup later on!'

By such comments the destinies of thousands are decided! It was said without, perhaps, very much thought beyond the moment—but it was meant sincerely. I could see, or thought I could see, how a bright spark like that would enjoy the fun and bustle of the group. Why, that would almost be therapy in itself!

But now I was not so sure. By the time Felicity was three years old her physical condition was evident to all. What had been just a medical term was now a visible disability. She had little voluntary movement in her arms and legs and the greatest difficulty in holding her head upright. But she was still as bright as a button. Her speech was sharp and articulate and her mother assured me she took an active interest in everything. So I promised her I would keep my word. I would have her in the group. And today was the day of reckoning.

I swung open the white gate in a gesture of welcome, greeting her mother with a smile and Felicity with a 'Hello little button!'

'I think you've made it just in time,' I added as the first raindrops splashed down heavily, making the children in the garden rush for the cover of the Coach House and shriek with excitement. Was it my imagination, or did the mother look just a little anxiously at the gaggle of running, excited children pushing past her and her helpless bundle as we, too, moved towards the door?

I had, of course, asked her to stay for the morning. I felt that Felicity would need all the experienced help she could get and her mother had a four-year start on the rest of us. We intended to do all that we could but a calm, organized, experienced mum was vital—that was obvious.

I noticed almost at once that, although she could not hold her head up well, Felicity was taking an interest. In fact she was drinking it all in, her eyes glancing here and there with an expression of intense excitement. We sat her down in a high-backed chair and, on her mother's instructions, padded her all round with cushions. She looked pretty secure—even regal—on her throne as she surveyed the exciting scene before her with evident relish. I relaxed a little. It was going to be all right. She was enjoying herself—as any child would.

In front of her we put a table to rest her frail hands on. Her feet, which were quite immobile, we put on a box underneath. For a few minutes she contented herself playing with a puzzle fitted with big knobs which even her weak fingers could manipulate. I moved off, determined to show everyone that I regarded the whole thing as entirely normal.

I didn't get very far before she brought me to a halt.

'It's not very sensible of you to put me here where I can't see what's going on in the play house!' she declared loudly. We agreed that she had a point. She was moved closer. I moved off again.

A few minutes later she commented stridently: 'I often drop things because my fingers don't work very well. Someone should sit near me to pick them up, please!'

This, again, sounded reasonable and so a 'slave' (there were several volunteers) was appointed to fetch and carry what she couldn't do for herself. And what a lot he had to do! For Felicity had taken over with a vengeance. Everyone within commenting distance was on the receiving end of some sharply worded (and sharply observed) comment.

'You are silly—*anyone* can see that should be the other way round!' she shot at a boy working on a shapes-box puzzle. He complied and the shape rattled successfully into the box. He smiled in appreciation. She smiled back.

'You can't cook things in a kettle!' she continued sharply—suddenly spotting a domestic inaccuracy in the culinary fantasy taking place in the now-visible play house. 'They *must* go in a pan!' explained the self-appointed cook-overseer, as four red bricks were hurriedly tipped from kettle to wooden saucepan and placed on the painted hob.

'S'better,' she confirmed, thrusting a large-knobbed piece of her own puzzle shakily home, as if to emphasize the point. It wobbled out.

'Pick that up please!' she called. The 'slave' leaped to obey. This was fun.

I smiled broadly to myself, relief and delight mingling on my face and in my heart. I imagined a serious-minded professional educationalist or doctor quizzing me about Felicity: 'And *integration*, Mrs Wyatt? Any problems with integration?'

With a gravity to match his own, I replied: 'I'm afraid so: becoming part of the group took her something over . . . *thirty seconds*!'

Felicity, like the summer rain lashing down outside, had taken the place by storm!

From that day on her observations and suggestions came thick and fast.

'Why don't we have "band" today?' So we did.

'Brian is doing something silly in the corner!' And he was.

'We should all be outside—the sun's out now!' And of course it was.

We were all thrilled at her active involvement —

interference even—in the life of the playgroup.
Though there was one thing we still dreaded—
the unthinking—and often hurtful—honesty of
children.

One day it happened. It was during a toileting
session and Filly, as we now called her, was propped
up on the long wooden bench by the wash basins,
drying her wet hands we had just dabbled in the
warm soapy water. Her floppy fingers could barely
hold the towel and her slave-for-the-day (the perky
daughter of the local fish and chip shop proprietor)
suddenly piped up:

'Filly, just look at your legs. They're not doing
anything again. What's the matter with them?'

All the helpers within earshot reacted as if light-
ning had just struck the Coach House roof. We
stood rooted to the spot and held our collective
breaths.

Felicity's face puckered up. We knew the worst
had happened. But we had reckoned without
Felicity's strong personality. She was angry, not an-
guished.

Abruptly she handed over the towel and waved an
admonishing finger.

'You listen to me! There's nothing wrong with my
legs. My brain' (and here the finger waved at her
head) 'is trying to send messages down to my legs to
tell them what to do; but because a lot of my muscles
don't work properly the nerves can't get the message
through, that's all!'

The slave paused for a moment, digesting this. It
was a complication in life that had not occurred to her
before.

'Oh, well,' she concluded, 'mine just walk!'

And that was that. We breathed again. Filly, we

could see, had a lot fewer problems in some areas
than many adult people we could think of.

But Felicity's understanding of her problems
didn't make them go away and, bright though she
might be, she still had to face a future which included
the assessment of doctors and the blinkered view
some of them have with regard to handicap.

The time came for her to move on to school. The
doctor assessed her and, although very impressed
with her verbal skills, decided—naturally—that she
should go to a school for severely physically handicapped children.

Her parents visited the school. It was a depressing
place. Most of the children there were multiply
handicapped and certainly didn't have the bright
enquiring, commanding mind of our Filly. It was an
old building, with few facilities, and only part-time
physiotherapy was available.

What earthly good could she gain from attending
this place? What about the local infants' school near
her home? She now had an electric wheelchair,
would need very little help in the classroom—except
at toilet time—and could certainly learn as fast as the
others. In addition, her big sister was there already.

The Local Education Authority's adviser and the
Medical Officer gave the matter a moment's thought
. . . and refused permission. We thought of Manchester High School for Girls. My daughter went
there at the time and felt that they might be rather
more enlightened. She was right. A place was offered
and we were all delighted. But it was a Direct Grant
school—who would pay?

Once again the Local Authority drew back. The
parents continued to lobby and eventually squeezed
out of them the major concession that she could have

a fortnight's trial at the school of our first choice—the local infants' school. That, they were sure, would soon show all of us how unrealistic our ideas were. And, of course, they insisted, her mother was to be in attendance the whole time. After all, the teacher had the other children to attend to.

So Felicity steamed in, with mother in tow.

After ten days the teacher had seen enough.

Not only had Felicity re-arranged the classroom but she had also done the same with the curriculum! The teacher wasn't just happy for her to stay—she simply couldn't bear the thought of losing her!

Felicity went from strength to strength—except in the area of muscles. She became a Brownie, a swimmer—well, floater really, and developed an instinctive taste for good fashion and design, plus a very mature, enquiring mind.

She was also a terror on two wheels—and her wheelchair had four. I stopped her once, racing down the pavement (she was then aged about seven) and told her to be careful in case she had an accident. She said I was not to worry. She'd had one once. She'd wondered what it would be like to be blind. So she'd shut her eyes while driving along, hit the kerb and been catapulted right out! She assured me she was much more careful now. I remained unconvinced.

She was bright, all right. In fact she eventually left the local comprehensive school with four 'A' levels and went on to college to study art.

We loved her very much—but it would be untrue to say that we weren't rather relieved when she moved on from the playgroup to school—and not only because we needed the rest! We recognized, despite the success, what I had known from the very start: that none of us was properly trained to work with handicapped children and we had simply been doing our best—along with her parents, who had given us constant help and encouragement.

As far as the playgroup was concerned we should mark it down as a little success story—one we could be proud of—and that was that.

But there were two things I didn't know then that I know now. We were welcoming a total of some eighty children to the playgroup through the white ranch gate (we had different children on alternate days, to meet the demand). And at that time the statistics for handicapped children in the UK stated that for every 100 children born alive two would be handicapped. In addition, at least three in every 100 would show signs of severe impairment before they reached play-school age. This meant that, on average, we should be seeing two or three handicapped children like Felicity regularly coming along to the group.

Where were they? I had made no restrictions on attendance. It did not occur to me even to ask. I simply didn't know.

The other thing I didn't know was that people had been watching our little unconsidered experiment with Felicity, and word was getting out.

One of the many uncomfortable things I have dis-covered over the years about work with handicapped children is that their parents have to learn what it is to wait.

In fact they seem to spend most of their lives waiting. Waiting for cars or ambulances, waiting for appointments, waiting for treatments, waiting for appliances to be fitted. And, since most of them are waiting together—most often in that aptly named social venue the 'waiting-room', they tend to talk, sharing their fears, hopes and worries.

'Hear about that floppy little girl . . . couldn't walk . . . got into an ordinary school though . . . up Heaton Moor way, wasn't it?'

'Heard she went to a playgroup. Carlton Road, I think. Who? Mrs Wyatt? Really? Oh! Mm.'

As I said, there were two things I didn't then know: an unpalatable statistic and some, often, pretty desperate people who, forced to wait, started to talk. Both factors were to become very significant to the playgroup, to those involved with it and, fundamentally, to me. The arrival of Felicity was a watershed that changed many things—completely.

But how did I come to be running a playgroup in the first place? For that we need to go back before the Coach House—way back in fact to my arrival in Stockport, just after the Second World War.

Chapter Two

GETTING STARTED

If I had been given any choice I'd have wanted to live somewhere far from big city strife, somewhere with a view of sweeping countryside, distant sea and tree-lined slopes—wouldn't most of us? I settled in Manchester because of John.

I met John one evening towards the end of the War. I was attending a meeting at the home of some Christian friends. In those dangerous years, with deeply thoughtful, committed Christian men like C. S. Lewis speaking often on the BBC about the importance and relevance of the Christian faith and with violent death a close reality for so many thousands of young people, an awareness of God in the person of Jesus Christ meant a great deal. Christ certainly became a brightly burning hope to many in the darkness of war. He was to John, I discovered. But there was still a need to discuss such things as belief in God, the truth of the Christian faith, the purpose of life . . . So our friends provided the opportunity for a meal and a meeting—to look at the Bible and to share experiences. Soldiers from the nearby camps came too—partly to listen to the discussions, and partly, I'm sure, to meet the girls. We did not object *too* much!

John and I were both Christians when we met, though very young and inexperienced. I was just beginning a degree course at Manchester University, and John, his heart set on civil engineering, was a young engineer in the army 'for the duration'. I liked him immediately, though he soon disappeared from the group as he was sent overseas on active service. I wondered if I would see him again.

I was fortunate for, unlike so many, he did return. But what he had seen had changed him. I had first met a lanky boy in uniform, now he was a strong and mature man. The horrors of war had only served to deepen his faith in Christ.

We were married and John enthusiastically set to work to master his profession—skills now so badly needed to rebuild bombed and stricken cities.

He chose to study in Manchester and, when he qualified, his local knowledge led him to continue in the area. We therefore settled just outside the city, in Stockport. I went out to teach, having graduated in French and then (a most unusual step in those days) taken a diploma in Nursery Education. To be honest we both wanted a family and the year's nursery education course seemed to me the best way to 'get trained' for the job! Then followed a revealing year teaching in inner Manchester before I left to give birth to our first child, Elisabeth.

We moved from a small flat to a little house, just by the main railway line from London to Manchester. Many were the mornings when our breakfast conversations were interrupted by the whoosh of (steam) express trains whistling through the cutting outside our front door, as they shut off steam for their approach to Stockport station.

Soon we had a son, John Stephen, and then

another daughter, Ruth. I did my best impression of 'supermum' amid the chaos of those mornings, as the young family prepared to meet the day with the inevitable mixture of arms, legs, shirts, socks, breakfast, cajolings, combings and last-minute tying of shoelaces. But no matter how late we were, we always did one thing: we paused for a time of prayer. Not for long—but just to give the day over to God. We still do, though all our children have long since flown the nest.

One morning, after I had waved the last of the family round the bend in the road, I sat down with baby Ruth and voiced an idea that had floated into my mind during the morning prayer.

'Ruth, I think God has been telling me something. Here I am all alone with you in a big room and no one else to play with! Now that doesn't seem right, does it? What we need are some friends. Now supposing mummy were to have some children round to play?'

Ruth thought that God had given mummy a very good idea indeed—and the very first friend should be Charlotte from next door who always needed someone to play with.

Being a nursery teacher, I thought it would be best if I formalized the whole thing and started a proper 'playgroup'. The idea was catching on all over the country. There would surely be lots of mums who would like to take up such an opportunity.

I cornered John about it that night and he seemed quite happy with the idea, even though it meant making over one—in fact the largest—of our downstairs rooms to accommodate the project. But he couldn't deny that it was, in every sense, a good idea.

He pointed out, though, that I would need to get permission—clearance and accreditation—from the Local Authority. I promised to do so and next day made the contact. They were helpful and glanced through the relevant by-laws. It seemed the room would need inspecting and the floor measuring: the law required something like twenty-five square feet of floor space per child. That sounded a lot to me but I went ahead and booked for the inspector to come. The lady, a doctor, arrived and approved the room, plus the bathroom too for good measure.

Then she asked about the floor space.

I had no idea how big the room was nor, come to that, how to measure it. I was a French graduate, not a mathematician.

'Not to worry,' she said, and produced a dress-maker's tape measure. 'We'll do it in squares.'

So we did.

Measuring the length and breadth of the room and dividing by the required area might have been simpler—as John pointed out when he got home—but our way was much more fun, and anyway, what did a civil engineer know about playgroups?

After some deliberation the doctor and I agreed on twelve children as a maximum. I was pleased. It seemed a handy number to me—and satisfied the requirements.

Now it was time to find the children. I decided to do something simple and advertise in the local press. The advertisement went in—and I sat by the phone. In my hand I had a brand-new register with a list of twelve places—the top two filled in with 'Ruth and Charlotte', followed by ten empty spaces.

The first dozen copies of the paper can hardly have been delivered that afternoon when the phone rang. Somewhat nervously I answered, trying my best to sound like the 'professional teacher' as advertised. It was a woman's voice.

'Oh, ah, Mrs Wyatt?' The hyper-cultured tone caused me to sit upright in my seat.

'Ah, could you tell me please, is your playgroup already full?'

I glanced down at the blank spaces in front of me.

'Ah, no-oo, not quite,' I countered.

A blast of honest northern relief greeted my reply and the voice dropped both its cool and its culture.

'Thank God. Then you can 'ave the little devil!'

I had my first customer.

Well, of course, I hadn't actually met her yet. But I was soon about to, as she dropped round right away to secure her place for the little 'horned horror' who turned out to be a lovely girl with blonde bunches.

I took the 'little devil' on and, within a week, I had nine others plus my special twosome—and a waiting-list. I was in business—a part of the playgroup movement which boomed in the sixties.

Chapter Three
LAYING FOUNDATIONS

The playgroup got off to a good start. John made a number of sturdy little tables (so sturdy we're still using them!) for the children to use for painting and drawing. Then we took everything else out of the large bow-windowed front room that had been approved for my chosen twelve. There were lots of toys and games and, generally, the children had a wonderful time. I found out (if I hadn't known it already) that I was really a frustrated actress at heart and the opportunity to play music, mime songs and tell stories was just what *I* enjoyed—never mind the children.

Of course, I'd taught before, and knew what I was about—though I reckoned that the nursery school in Manchester where I had served my apprenticeship had proved more of an education to me than to anyone else. But having my own little school in my own home was quite different. And I could see by the waiting-list that I was meeting a real need. These young mums had grown up during the Second World War. Now, with a whole new set of values and hopes for their marriages and families, they were desperate to meet other mothers and children, to find common causes and experiences. They needed to reassure themselves that their noisy little 'devils' were quite normal after all. The pre-war family and community that would have provided all this support was now dispersed to a large degree, and I could see that the playgroup was providing a much needed 'something' in its stead.

As the playgroup went on, I found myself becoming involved with the needs and concerns of the mothers as well as the children. I have always loved to chat to people and was around anyway when the children were collected. Without my becoming aware of it, a lot unfolded before me in snippits and chats. I didn't know it, in those early days, but I was learning—and drawing conclusions. I had seen the deprivation of inner city life, and I was discovering the deprivations, often emotional not physical, of suburban life. I can see now that what I discovered, simply by listening and chatting, formed the basis of convictions that would colour my whole future.

The grim, dedicated greyness of the fifties was about to burst into the boisterous confidence of the sixties. It was a time when the 'family' values which had been so vital for seeing out the war and its aftermath, seemed suddenly outdated and wide open to attack. The young—and that included the young mums I knew—looked at things from a radically different perspective from that of their forebears, as I did myself.

Society had changed. This was the generation of the 'brave new world' for the heroes of the war to live in. Much of it was very good indeed. Freely on offer (as never before) were Education, Social Services, National Health provision—the three pillars of post-war hope. Knowledge, concern, good health — it was heady stuff. Surely with these things put on a proper footing Britain would really be *great* at last.

But, wonderful though these free services were, I began to see that other things were still needed to make a community work. These were not things that could simply be taught in schools, administered socially or prescribed as medicine. They were the intangibles—courtesy, discipline, respect for parents, fidelity, trust, honesty, human worth—values which had been upstaged by the magic of science and the adventurous freedom of new thinking.

What was new was attractive, seemingly powerful and effective. The old style was a long way out.

It *was* an exciting age. Perhaps for the first time; women had access not only to qualifications but to the same careers as men. Within the family the father was still generally accepted as the one who went out to work (though the winds of change were already blowing). But wives now also understood the world of work and a mother might nurture her own ambition and hopes for a career outside the home.

To those whose hopes of a career had been interrupted (if not prevented) by marriage, the subsequent arrival of children was a major inconvenience which was at times almost too much to bear. What was she, with her fully trained mind, doing in charge of an insatiable little creature who bawled all day long? Where was the clean precision of the chemistry lab or the quiet relaxation of the common-room? Sacrificed to the rearing of children—something that surely 'anyone' could do!

And yet, although enlightened, educated and emancipated, the women of Heaton Moor—our suburb of Stockport—often found themselves a generation sadly unprepared for the realities of bringing up children. How was it done? What was required of them? What values should they look for to guide their own offspring? What *was* their responsibility? And what about meeting their own needs as women? These questions are still being asked today.

And so, slowly, through meeting the mums, using my training with the children, and talking things over continually (as well as praying about them), I began to realize that the values of family life which I held as a Christian, that often seemed so 'dated' when set against the modern ideas and excitements, were still needed—and needed badly. They were needed *alongside* the benefits of education, welfare and the health service. Without the positive control afforded by these other principles, this state machinery could easily veer wildly off course.

These are the beliefs that have motivated my work and concern for young children and families, more latterly those with handicapped children, over the years from those early beginnings to the present day. They are still fundamental if the family is to survive.

Perhaps it seems rather grand to say all of this 'understanding' came out of a simple children's playgroup, meeting the mums and working with the children. But I am often asked today by students, doctors, social workers and teachers about the principles which have guided the work I have been involved in for over twenty-five years—and which are now being taken up by others. I acknowledge my debt to people like Brofenbrunner and Kellmer Pringle, well-known and effective thinkers on the subject. But then I have to pause and confess that as a Christian who takes the teaching of the Bible seriously I find the bases all there. They're not really so new. I work on the principle that people, whatever

their condition, matter to God and have need of him.
If they matter to him, they must matter to me. The
values of human worth, family love and personal
respect are God's values. And it is not just a matter of
it working for *me*, as some people think. It's simply
that it *works*.

Just *how* it works is the best part of the story.

With three fast-growing children of our own, plus
a dozen morning visitors, we began to feel that it was
time to move into a bigger house. I got it into my head
that it would have to be a large old house. Large: for
the family, the playgroup and for meetings we held at
home to do with our local church. Old: because it
seemed to me that was the only sort we were going to
get on John's junior civil engineer's income. We
would of course try to do it up. John would be good at
that, I knew—with his background in buildings and
structures.

As it turned out, John's expertise was often called
on. Each old wreck I found for sale on my daily walks
round the nearby streets he would dutifully go and
take a look at. He would prod here and there, lean on
a few things and then quietly pronounce the death
sentence on my hopes.

There was always something wrong. And always
so major that there was no chance of our even con-
sidering it.

'Galloping dry rot,' he would say. 'Everywhere.'

That was very common. Around Heaton Moor
galloping dry rot was not only endemic, it was so bad
you could almost hear the horses coming!

'Subsidence undermining the foundations,' he
would continue. Or: 'Joists seem to be held up by the
roof here.'

I began to realize that my dream of finding a big old house was going to stay just that—a dream.

We had proved time and time again that God cared for us and had a plan for our lives, so naturally we prayed about it—and I continued to walk the streets looking for the house.

I knew it was out there somewhere, if only I could find it.

Chapter Four

CHARNWOOD

It was in early spring that I saw the notice.

The first of the mad March gales had swept in from a storm-tossed Irish Sea and, working itself into an angry lather over the jagged hills of North Wales, had rushed inland to buffet vengefully at the windows of our little house near the railway, before whistling ineffectually onwards through the Victorian stone archways of the Stockport viaduct. When I went out, the streets were strewn with the debris of blown twigs lying scattered on the pavement, snapping and catching in the wheels of Ruth's pushchair as we went along.

'New Houses for Sale,' the notice said. These were unknown in our district since before the war.

I looked round but all I could see was a rather dismal old one: Dean House—a ramshackle old mansion that we, or rather John, had long since condemned.

The door was open and there was the sound of work going on. Perhaps someone was refurbishing it. Maybe this was what we were looking for. I went in to investigate but could see no one. I shouted up to the workmen hammering and banging upstairs.

'Just where are all these new houses for sale, then?'

A regional reply floated down from above.

'Right here, luv'—when we've got this old feller down!'

'Oh, here? What kind are you going to build— would you build one for us?' I shouted back. To this day I do not know what possessed me to say that. Though, looking back, I can clearly see God's hand in it all. Anyway, I had the man's interest. Soon I had his address as well, and had set up a meeting with him and an architect he knew, for the following Sunday.

Then I had to tell John. I knew very well that purpose-built new houses were not something that would normally fall into his line of thinking (or present income), to put it mildly. The more I thought about what I'd done, the worse it got. I didn't even go home, but called him from the next phone-box and spilt the beans all in a rush.

'Darling, I've just met a builder and they're putting up some houses in Dean Road and I've asked him to come over to us and quote us a price for one and that's going to be next Sunday . . .'

Then I stopped and caught my breath. John is very firm when he wants to be. Seven years in the army leave their mark.

'That's all right, darling,' he said. And, by the way he said it, I knew at once that he didn't mind! I was amazed.

And so it all went ahead. The builder and architect arrived as agreed and we outlined our ideas. The young architect showed us some of his plans—which included a very large lounge, ideal for our youth group meetings—and the builder started making some estimates. I saw the architect glancing all the time at our bookshelf, which was stuffed to over- flowing with Christian books and paperbacks.

'You must be Christians,' he commented during the proceedings. We said we were. He had worked with someone who had that kind of belief, he said, though he did not understand it himself—and the discussion went on. Then he asked if he might have a private word with the builder in the hall. In a few moments he came back in and gave us a quote.

Before we could answer, he added: 'My solicitor would be willing to fund the initial building on the basis that Mr Wyatt supervises the construction himself, professionally. I know this is unusual, but we trust that you are sincere people. Our estimate is based accordingly.'

The quote was—what do they say?—highly competitive? 'Rock bottom' would be my choice. But I knew that with John supervising there would be no skimping on the job.

We promptly got cold feet. This was too good to be true. Surely they were leading us on? But no, these were men of local repute talking honest business. We, too, had to do some trusting.

We accepted—and the house was built in six months flat. Our old house was sold, unexpectedly quickly, to a family we met through the church. They were having to move house, but wanted to stay in the area. There was 'just nothing about' they told us. We soon pointed out their mistake; and so the moves were complete.

But what of the playgroup in all this? After all, that was one of the reasons I had wanted to move in the first place. The plan showed the dining-room of our new house leading directly out to the garden, right next to the kitchen, so we included on the plans an additional 'sun-room' annexe, which would be built onto the wall outside.

There I could have twenty children each morning instead of twelve—and the garden gave us somewhere for them to play outside during their mid-morning break. I could also take on part-timers. One group could come Mondays, Wednesdays and Fridays, and the other Tuesdays and Thursdays. So we could cater for about forty children all told.

We called the house—and the playgroup—'Charnwood', after a favourite childhood haunt of John's: a forest in Leicestershire. There, as a young man, he had made a vital step of faith and commitment as a Christian, and it seemed right to us to acknowledge God's goodness in our new home. So 'Charnwood Nursery Group' re-opened on 10 September 1959, the start of the winter term.

One of the greatest gifts I think God gave us in the early days of Charnwood was the gift of people. And not just in the early days, but all along the way. Today, our skilled staff are our greatest asset. (Among them are several who have been both parents and colleagues.) But I am thinking of one person in particular who turned up then very much as a gift— and something of a messenger too—from God, and who has stayed with us ever since.

It was after the birth of our fourth child. For obvious reasons I'd had to close the playgroup just before the baby was due. I was rather afraid that this closure might well extend to years rather than months, for my usual helper had just been diagnosed as having a serious heart condition and could not possibly run the show alone. As for myself, I knew from experience that I would be too occupied with the new baby to be of any practical use for some time to come. But baby Timothy was due 1 August and arrived on 1 August—and he soon began to show he was that sort of boy. So with this good-natured, ultra-convenient baby I soon got round to wondering if the playgroup would not be possible after all. Once again, I prayed about it.

A day or two later, the phone rang.

'Oh, Mrs Wyatt, you won't know me but I'm calling concerning the vacancy for staff at your playgroup.'

Vacancy, I thought? What vacancy? I had not yet restarted the group, let alone advertised for staff. I was about to put this rather presumptuous caller off, when I suddenly remembered—I had prayed for help!

'Of course; how kind of you to phone. Please do come round.'

She did, and in a matter of minutes we became aware that we shared many interests. Erica Vere has worked with me ever since. Later I discovered that she was a member of the Society of Friends (the Quakers) and shared our Christian faith, if from a different perspective.

So, with Erica's help, I took the plunge and re-opened. Local mothers were delighted and soon the waiting-list boomed. As before, we made a point of interesting and involving the parents in the activities of their children. Charnwood was no morning dumping-ground for the mothers' convenience! We also had, I believe, a genuine interest in the families. We wanted to know and help, if we could.

Sometimes some of the mums came back early, in time for the final sing-song or story time. In this way they picked up ideas about home play-time and stories for their children.

Others, by contrast, were always late in picking up their offspring.

There was Dan's mum: though to be fair it wasn't really his mum who did the collecting. Dan was nearly always left waiting around several minutes after the others had gone. But he wouldn't be listening for a car. He would wait and listen for a deep-throated 'woof woof'—the only warning we got that the family hound, Rufus, was about to put in a breathtaking appearance. Breathtaking if he landed on you, that is. He was generally followed closely by a totally breathless mum who, we always felt, had been brought along by the dog to ensure she got the exercise.

'Er, don't . . . you . . . mind . . . him, Mrs Wyatt,' she gasped, wrestling with the lead, on our first meeting. 'He's a'right! Ex-police dog is Rufus—he's only gun-shy—just right for our pub.'

I always felt that Dan and the pub where he lived were in safe hands, or paws—and I'm glad that Rufus never caught me being anything but the most tender-hearted teacher where little Dan was concerned.

Animals as well as mums always seemed to feature strongly in the closing proceedings. I remember Emma and Louise, whose mother, in order to pacify Louise, permitted her to bring Loftus and Shortcake along with her to join the group. These were a pair of very fine tortoises, whose only problem seemed to be one of relationships. They hated the sight of each other.

I did what I could, but they obviously felt it best that all aggression came out into the open, and thus the playgroup was required to endure the sound of a continual clashing of shells, accompanied by miscellaneous hissings and snortings. This was not too bad until it came to the closing story time, which for some of the children was a matter of serious concentration. More often than not 'L' and 'S' had to be removed, so that they could continue their titanic struggle in the garden and give us the required peace and quiet.

Then there was Roddy. His father was a local doctor and Roddy took after him, in that from an early age he was very keen on investigating the limits of physical phenomena. Choosing himself as the most interesting and immediate subject, he would usually take the opportunity, while Dad was delayed at the surgery, to engage in the 'Door-swing Dash Demo'—the most energetic of his trials—and possible only when the house was largely clear of other children. It involved first going into our kitchen and fully opening the fridge door, which was on a slow hinge. This was, as it were, the starting-gun. He would then leap across the kitchen, dart out through the back door, round the house, in through the sun-room side door, up through the dining-room and back to the kitchen, hoping to catch the fridge door before it closed. Being of only modest athletic ability, he never made it—but, since the test was the thing, this was of no consequence and merely gave him the unassailable excuse to do it over and over again.

Roddy is now a research analyst with computers, and my fridge and I are prepared to take a lot of the credit for laying down the firm foundations of his present career!

There was a lot of fun, quite a few scrapes, and tears, too, as our experience grew. Many of the incidents were trivial and funny, but sometimes things went deeper, occasionally touching the very basis of our beliefs and convictions.

There was a little red-haired girl called Mandy. One day, during picture-book time, she came across an unpleasant drawing. It was a rather graphic illustration of Jesus on the cross. I was shocked myself that such a violent illustration should be in a child's book that someone had given to the playgroup. It was in no way appropriate for a three-year-old. But the damage had been done. Mandy was very disturbed, and I had to calm the child's natural horror.

I took her aside and told her that the picture wasn't from a fairy story, and that the man on the cross was really a good man who had loved little children and had made lots of sick people better, but in spite of this people had killed him. I explained that it was all right in the end. God had made him alive again because he loved him very specially. More than that, I felt, would be beyond her.

After I'd finished, I mopped her eyes with a tissue, and a dim little smile lit up her round, tear-stained face.

'Oh, that's lovely,' she sighed. 'I'm going to tell my mummy about that man.'

I was pleased, both with her smile and with the fact that I had been able to recover the situation and yet be truthful. Next morning, however, back came Mandy, looking very grim indeed. Arms akimbo, she stood in the doorway.

'Mummy says it's not true,' she opened shortly. For a moment I could not recall what on earth I'd said that her mother might find incredible.

'Oh, about Jesus?' I ventured.

'Yes,' she said. 'It's not true what you said! He never came back. He's still dead!'

I was a little shaken by her vehemence but I could hardly agree. However, I had to be careful here. It is normally a firm rule at Charnwood that 'mothers know best'. So I started to explain as simply as I knew

how that the evidence for Jesus rising from the grave
was pretty convincing. I told her about the disciples
who had seen him, and had had fish for breakfast at a
picnic by the lake. I mentioned others who had seen
him too. Perhaps her mummy just hadn't had time to
look into all this, I suggested. I was sure I had made
my point—offering helpings of resurrection theology
to three-year-old minds is not something I have done
a lot of, but she certainly seemed impressed and said,
'Oh, I'll tell Mummy that.' Nevertheless, I had a
shrewd suspicion what the result might be.

I was right. The next day, back came Mandy again
with: 'He's still dead, Mummy says so!'

'I'm sorry Mandy,' I said, 'but he truly is alive—
I've just been talking to him. It's called praying.'
Then I promptly changed the subject—not wanting
to undermine either my own, or her mother's relationship with the child.

Nothing further happened until a few days later,
when her mother dropped by with a petition for me
to sign. That was a surprise in itself, because I had
been getting the feeling she was avoiding me. Trying
to break the ice I commented as I signed her sheet:
'I'm so glad you are doing this. I'm sure you're right
to protest, but I have to confess I'm also glad that my
future doesn't rest in the hands of any human government.'

She took the point straight away.

'I know what you mean and in a way I'm sorry for
contradicting you about what you told Mandy. But,
well, things have been very difficult for us recently.'

She went on to tell me that they had been a church-
going family until her father had been taken ill with
cancer. Dying in hospital, he asked the minister to
visit him there. But when he arrived, he wouldn't sit

near her father's bed or even take his hand, which
upset him deeply. She felt it showed a hollow faith.

'I saw then that the whole thing was just a sham. If
he'd trusted a real God he wouldn't have been afraid
to go near my dad, would he? Well, Dad died and
we've not been back to church since,' she concluded
abruptly.

I realized she had been sadly let down. But then,
how often have I done the same, letting down people
who had expected my faith to show through? I was
chastened to think of it. We talked for a while and I
persuaded her to have a look for herself at what the
Bible said. She confessed she had never looked at it
before and I gave her a New Testament in modern
English to read. We parted on a note of deeper
understanding—for both of us. She moved away
shortly after, so I never knew if what I had done was
of any help. But we had both learned something
important—all because a child at Charnwood had
picked up the wrong book.

In all, those first few years were busy ones, and
there was a great deal for us to discover. But I was
delighted. God had given me a home, a family and all
the interest of this link with mothers and children.
My work was clear, my future laid out. Which only
goes to show just how much I had to learn!

Chapter Five

'THE COACH HOUSE'

I emitted a cry. It was quiet and half stifled but a cry nevertheless, and John heard it from the next room. He came in at once and looked at me. I put out a hand to steady myself and offered him the letter.

It bore the headed crest of the Stockport Borough Council, Town Clerk's Office. The contents were direct and uncompromising. The heading summed it up: PUBLIC NUISANCE, Dean Road.

The paragraphs that followed detailed the 'here-to-fores' and 'here-in-unders' but the heart of the text had been kept to a minimum in order to convey the essential message that, as a consequence of complaints, I and my playgroup were considered to be a Public Nuisance—and were to desist. Forthwith.

They were closing us down. Immediately.

Well, perhaps not quite. What was required was an official visit to the Town Hall, for me to offer an explanation. But as the Town Clerk said when we met later that day:

'Your activities with the children are the cause of several complaints. Your playgroup must close.'

We closed that night. It was all so sudden that I had to greet parents the next morning, as they drove up in their cars (this was one of the things that had offended the neighbours) to drop their little ones off, with the news that there was no playgroup for them to come to. It was a bitter experience, and it came right on top of a family tragedy. John's mother, who was elderly, had been staying with us for the winter. One night, imagining in her own mind that there was a lonely child in the garden, she had climbed out of an upstairs window to help. She fell from the flat roof of the playroom onto the side alleyway—and died in hospital just a few hours later. The horror of her accident was as disturbing to me as the death itself. And the closing of the playgroup—which had now been running successfully for four years—was not only a blow to me but an affront to the community. It mattered to me that I was able to help and now it seemed as though even this had been denied me.

I was confused by what had happened and angry too that God had allowed it. All I had done seemed an extravagance. Even our large house with its extension for the playgroup—which had made things very tight on John's income—even that was all wasted now.

It was a time of stress and anxiety and my health deteriorated. A few days in hospital were followed by a recommendation to take a complete rest. I did my best, though we now had four children—and John did what he could. Slowly the pressure seemed to ease. My prayers became more coherent and the direction once again became clear—I must ask for the right place to start all over again. Our personal problems had not lessened the need for a playgroup.

I must confess I was tempted for a short while to try and re-open the playgroup where I was. The lovely sunroom stood empty and the toys and equipment almost seemed to mock me. When we had

closed, several of the fathers who worked for a
national newspaper had offered to do a full feature on
our plight. I knew that they would make a good job of
it and for all I knew could put enough pressure on the
Town Hall to get them to rescind their closure order.
But community spirit was what we valued—and
what I thought God valued. If we just set up again
there would only be more complaints from neighbours, some of whom were elderly; and their needs
were just as important as the needs of our children. I
said thank you, but no.

I really had done all I could. John and I decided we
must wait (as we said) for guidance.

Not long after, I received a call from a local dentist.
He had been one of the playgroup fathers and knew
the problem. It seemed he had acquired a piece of
property for a new surgery in the Moor area and it
had a sort of coach house annexe, set in its own
garden.

'It's not in much shape,' he said, 'but, if it's any
use to you, come over and have a look at it.'

Naturally we were surprised—and cautiously en-
thusiastic, given that we had not seen the place. So
we agreed to go round and have a look. One obvious
advantage was that it was local. The mums who had
been disappointed by our closure were the ones who
would again be able to benefit.

It was in the evening, and dusk, when we kept our
appointment, so the coach house was difficult to see.
But I had a feeling about it, even as John and I looked
at it in the starlight. It had a little Edwardian-style
roof with crenellations all the way along the top
and, being a coach house, had two wide hayloft
apertures (now windows) and a big ground-level
coaching door, which gave the whole place the

appearance of a face.

'Almost a gingerbread house,' I said quietly. 'Right out of Hans Andersen's fairy tales.'

But I was talking to myself, because John and the dentist were already deep in conversation, and John was already into his standard line about the galloping dry rot (in a coach house of all places!), not to mention the damp sections and, of course, the doubtful strength of the upstairs hayloft flooring. Then there was some doubt over the stairs and . . .

I was disappointed in him. Couldn't he recognize a gift from God when he was shown one? What was the matter with him?

But he was doing some hard thinking. The estimated cost of renovation, to bring it anywhere near the standard we would want for our playgroup, was frightening. We hadn't a hope of getting money like that. He talked on, his professional comments irrefutable, since he had only to lift a floor-board or tap on the wall to confirm his observations. Added to which, he pointed out, it wasn't our property. Any money we put in for renovation would be lost at the end of the day. No, it was no good. The kind idea had promise but the whole thing just wouldn't work.

The dentist reflected.

'Well, I think the only alternative is for me to fund the improvements for you,' he said. 'Up to a maximum of . . .' and he quoted a sizeable sum. John still wasn't quite happy.

'I'd want a qualified architect to plan the improvements,' he said.

'Of course. You must do it properly.'

We decided to think about it.

Some time later the dentist and his wife came round to confirm their offer. They feared that perhaps we hadn't taken their offer of funding the improvements too seriously. To be honest, we hadn't.

No sooner had I opened the front door to them than the phone rang. It was a friend, Irene—a local mother and graduate teacher. Just the sort of person I would be desperate for if we did decide to go ahead with the coach house. She was too qualified in fact. It would be an insult even to ask her.

'Sorry to trouble you, Grace,' she opened. 'It's about your old playgroup. Well, I know you've got no premises for a new one, if you see what I mean—and I really have been praying about that of course . . .' She paused. 'No-o,' she added, half to herself. 'You'll think me mad, Grace.'

'Yes?' I encouraged, wanting only to join our guests, and very impatient to get the big decision over with.

'Well, I know it sounds silly, but I felt sure God wanted me to phone and offer my help, I mean as a teacher. When you start up again . . . if you do, that is . . . possibly. What do you think?'

So the work began. Although the sum for the improvements was quite generous, we knew that some extra work would still have to be done by us. But we set to with a will. The plans were drawn up and we went to work.

We weren't actually changing anything structurally. It was a matter of righting the wrongs that John had spotted: reinforcing the floor upstairs, letting more light through a new large window, installing proper toilet facilities—particularly small ones for the children—painting and decorating.

By far the most impressive operation was the installation of the piano. I insisted that the big upstairs

hayloft was the only room that would be suitable for
all the music and dancing and singing the children
would want to do—so upstairs it had to be. Well, the
stairs were too narrow, so John ordered a crane.
Gingerly we manoeuvred the piano through the upstairs window of the house and slid it gently into
position. I saw John wince a bit as the rafters took the
strain, but they held, and the piano was installed.

We knew just how important the piano was to the
little community we would be setting up every
morning at the playgroup—every child deserves
bright cheerful music in their lives—though I had no
idea then how much that instrument would come to
mean to one child in particular. But I am getting
ahead of myself.

Eventually the coach house itself was ready and we
turned to the garden. We needed a sandpit, so John
organized some boys from the local church to come
and dig one out. It was not just any sandpit. This one
needed *five tons* of sand to fill it when finished and had
concrete slabs all around for firm edging. Then we
needed a climbing-frame—and what about a swing?
Of course, there had to be a fence to keep the
children safe. And a gate, for the mums, our helpers
and me to lean on and chat. Was there no end to my
requirements?

Actually the gate was the last vital item. In fact it
was the gate that was to become the playgroup's
crowning glory. We had a large, white, wooden one
made, which looked as though it had been made for a
Mexican hacienda or Texan ranch. It rounded off
the garden and play area safely and in fine style and
soon came, in my mind, to be the 'gate' into many
people's lives as well as to the second home—known
to everyone as the Coach House—of Charnwood

Nursery Group. It was also the gate through which
Felicity, carried by her mother and escorted by her
sister, entered Charnwood, and our lives, that rainy
summer's day—leaving the impact of her coming
with us for ever.

Finally the day came for the grand opening and I
was thrilled to see the mums and dads arriving for the
first Monday morning, and to hear the 'oohs' and 'ahs'
of the children as they ran around the house and
garden. Downstairs there were now two brightly
painted rooms, one of them a cloakroom, and an
alcove for sticking pictures, for cutting and
colouring. Upstairs was simply one large airy room
for tumbling about and singing and dancing to
music, and outside there was the lovely secure garden
with real grass, trees and flowers (some of the
children had never played in this way before). There
were real animals too. Many a passing dog, cat or bird
suddenly became the surprised recipient of affection
in the shape of a bear hug or (for the birds) half a
lunchtime biscuit whizzing in their direction.

Fiona was one little girl who learned something
about trees. She joined us in September and on her
first morning went out to play in the sandpit. It
wasn't long before she came rushing back into the
Coach House. She grabbed my hand and dragged me
outside—over to a leafy apple tree by the pit, and
pointed up at the late summer fruit hanging from the
branches.

' 'Ere, who's been tyin' them apples up there?' she
demanded to know.

For a moment I was lost for words, wondering if
theology (God makes everything grow) or botany
(how he does it) was called for. Neither, I decided.

'They're not tied up there, Fiona. They *grow*

there,' I replied. 'It's an apple tree,' I continued carefully.

Fiona was disgusted at my ignorance.

'Don't you be daft! Apples come in boxes—I *know*. I've seen them!' Her father was the local green-grocer and the family lived over the shop!

I gave her ten-out-of-ten for observation.

The Coach House at Clifton Road was clearly a great success. We could handle double the number of children—eighty now—and Erica, Irene and I soon settled into a good working relationship. The whole thing was bigger and better than before, and parents were phoning up and writing all the time for their son or daughter to be put on the waiting-list.

Some parents were so keen on the playgroup that it seemed almost to be a matter of life and death.

One afternoon the doorbell rang at home, and there stood an elegantly dressed Indian. He intro-duced himself and enquired if I was the lady with 'the school'. Indeed I was, I assured him. He came in and sat down.

'Mrs Wyatt, I am wanting to come closer to you!'

Somewhat startled by this approach I asked, guardedly, for further explanation.

'Oh, it is too late for me—but I wish to have my son at your school. He will then grow very close to you!'

Light dawned. He was concerned for racial in-tegration within the community—not the essential attraction of my personality! I nodded approvingly.

'How old is your son?'

'Nine month!'

'Good,' I said. 'We'll be glad to have him at Charn-wood when he is three years old.'

He was shattered.

'Oh dear, dear me, not until he is three?'

I consoled him and encouraged him to contact us nearer the time when his son became eligible, assuring him that Sachu would meanwhile be put on the waiting-list.

Reluctantly he left.

Every month for the next nine months I received a phone call.

'Mrs Wyatt—are you ready now to receive Sachu to be with you?'

Every time I had to explain that Sachu was still too young.

'But Mrs Wyatt, what if his brain starts working and he is not with you?'

There was not a lot I could say to that.

When Sachu was about two, I had a bright idea and changed tack.

'What language does your son speak, Mr Joshi?'

'Gujurati, Mrs Wyatt.'

'Oh, what a pity, we have no one in the playgroup who can speak that. Please will you be kind enough to teach him English and *then* I'm sure he will be ready to join us.'

He was overjoyed.

Two weeks later he came round with his son— beautifully dressed for his 'interview'. He had learned English. Clearly Sachu was a bright boy.

Tiny and perfumed he stood, his big dark eyes gazing unblinkingly at me.

'Now Sachu, speak for Mrs Wyatt!'

His father pointed to the toy car his diminutive offspring clutched in his hand.

'What is that you have in your hand?'

'Broom, broom,' said Sachu.

'Oh, very good,' beamed his father. He made the

shape of a gun with his finger.

'Bang, bang,' responded Sachu, earnestly.

'Oh, excellent, Sachu,' confirmed his father. 'Such lovely English.' He turned to me gravely. 'And now he has one more word Mrs Wyatt—"wee wee"!'

Sachu joined Charnwood the next week. He was several months too young perhaps—but very well prepared!

Sachu was more than welcome—as were all the others, including Felicity when she came along. As things turned out hers was a great success story, something to be proud of. But there were a great many things I myself and all of us at Charnwood didn't know about handicapped children and their families—things we were about to find out . . . very soon. Very soon indeed.

Chapter Six

SHATTERING STATISTICS

Not long after Felicity had begun attending primary school, a lady wandered in through the white gate and up to the door of the Coach House. A child— rather large to be carried, I thought—was in her arms. I could see a mop of brown curly hair tied loosely with a purple ribbon.

I went out to greet them.

As I looked into the child's face I was shocked into silence. She had *no eyes*. A fold of skin covered each of the empty sockets. I shuddered and then, taking a firm grip on myself, asked to be introduced.

'This is Nina,' offered her mum.

'Hello, Nina,' I said as brightly as I could manage. The child wriggled a bit and her mouth curved, possibly into a smile. But she made no sound.

Her mother continued: 'I'm afraid she can't speak —though she seems to understand a few words. She's spastic too . . . and sometimes has fits. She can't stand or walk and I'm afraid she's not toilet trained. Would you have her here, though? You know—like Felicity.'

I was horrified by this matter-of-fact revelation of her staggering list of problems—clearly only too familiar to her mum.

'What happens to her now?' I asked, dazed. 'What help are you getting at the moment?'

'She goes twice a week to hospital for physiotherapy and the rest of the time she stays with me.'

The mother spoke on, urgently: 'I know there's a nursery for spastic children in Manchester but I don't want her to go there. She needs to hear normal children and learn—doesn't she, like Felicity did? Oh, *do* you think you could manage her? It looks so lovely here. You'd like it here, wouldn't you Nina?'

She hugged the child warmly. Nina wriggled, possibly excited at the prospect. Who knew? She turned her head a little at the noise of a shout from a child in the garden, then clung more tightly to her mother.

What could I say?

The other staff and helpers gathered round us and asked questions. Where did she live? Just up the road? Why hadn't we heard of her before? Surely the doctors had something more professional to offer than just 'physio' a couple of times a week and a spastic children's nursery three miles away?

Apparently not. Well, we were hardly qualified to help, were we?

Reluctantly, we asked Nina's mum to come back next week, when we'd had time to think it over.

Immediately we fell into a discussion which lasted off and on for the next few days, in fact weeks. What did we know about this sort of child? What were we supposed to know—as teachers and playgroup leaders? What were our responsibilities to the State? We really had no idea . . . And before God?

But the word was out, and the waiting-room jungle drums were beating.

A day or so later I was out playing with some of the children on the climbing-frame, trying to convince

them that space rockets need clinging onto—tightly—
even when you are on interplanetary rescue missions,
when I became aware of a lady watching us all,
closely, from over the white ranch gate.

I apologized for not noticing her earlier, and introduced myself.

'This is Nicholas,' said his mother, returning the
courtesy and indicating her cheerful-looking son,
whom she supported with, I thought, a particularly
firm arm.

'May I have a chat with you? If you've a moment,'
she added, nodding at the busy scene all around.

'Of course.'

We sat down together on the bench in the alcove.
It was quieter there. I showed Nicholas a wooden car,
and noticed immediately that without his mother's
support it was as much as he could do to sit up and his
stiff fingers just wouldn't—or couldn't—grasp the car.

Alarm bells began ringing inside my head.

'He has cerebral palsy,' admitted his mother. 'He
has severe motor difficulties and can't sit up unaided
or hold his head erect properly.'

Nicholas had spotted a drawing of a car and waved
his hands towards it and made a sound. She spoke out
straight away.

'Yes, Nicholas, a . . . CAR.' She repeated it, deliberately.

'He can't articulate properly, either—we have to
guess at what he means most of the time.'

At least, I thought to myself, this child can see. A
mental picture of sightless, handicapped little Nina
rose unbidden in my mind.

I questioned the mother further and discovered
that she had been a local schoolteacher—I had
guessed as much from her informed understanding

of Nicholas' condition—and that she lived just two streets away.

What help did she get from the hospital, etc, I asked?

Two sessions of physio each week, and the suggestion that he should go to the cerebral palsy nursery school in Manchester. Just the same as Nina—cerebral palsy was apparently the proper name for 'spastic'.

'I know he'll have to go to a special school later on but I'd so much like him to have the chance to see and be with normal children for a bit. If all he ever sees are handicapped children he'll never learn to mix with anyone 'normal'. None of the children at the other nursery can talk any better than he does. He'll never learn from them. And anyway it's so far . . .' She broke off. Her face was strained and exhausted.

'Could he come, Mrs Wyatt—even for a short time?'

By this time some of the children had come in from the garden to play more quietly. Two sat down near us and began colouring a chain of paper cut-out men. We watched them together, silently, for a moment or two. Then one little girl got up and showed Nicholas what she had done.

He grabbed out at the pretty coloured shapes and, before his mother could move to stop him, had caught one of them in his stiff unwieldy fingers. The girl, far from being unhappy, just laughed and sat down again to colour on, leaving Nicholas proudly waving them at his delighted mother.

He was actually *holding* the paper shapes.

Nicholas and his mother left with my promise—as in the case of Nina—that we would have to think about this very carefully but that she would have our answer as soon as possible.

After that morning's session was over I called a meeting of the staff and helpers and we discussed together this new request. All were alarmed to hear that he lived literally just down the road. As with Nina, no one had ever seen Nicholas before.

How many more handicapped children, we wondered, lived in our neighbourhood?

We looked around at the dear old building. Just a converted coach house—but a happy challenging environment for forty children each morning. But they were 'normal' children.

We really had no facilities for anyone handicapped: no main supply of hot water, no changing area for untoiletable children, no warm floors or supportive chairs for weak bones or bodies. Both mothers had offered full-time support and help. Their experience would be all we had to hand in any case—but were these handicapped children *our* responsibility?

We couldn't decide, and the decision was put off. We continued to talk and pray about the new requests—and each time Nina and Nicholas were brought to see us we made a little fuss of them—but we could offer no decision about a regular commitment. Each time it seemed we became more, not less, alarmed at the problems they presented.

I was also personally increasingly unhappy about my feelings towards these children. I felt mildly revolted and fearful whenever they were present— though I kept my feelings to myself as far as I could. I expect the mothers knew, though.

Above all I was ashamed. Did I really *want* to help?

Our own children were attractive and gifted. Nothing in my life, not even Felicity, had prepared me for the prospect of becoming involved and responsible for children with such severe needs.

I could see it was going to be no superficial business. Not just a matter of seeing the child each morning and sending him home at twelve. Though what with one thing and another we were more involved than that with our 'normal' children and their parents. But I could sense—and see—something of the deep commitment to the children and their families which was needed if we were ever to be of real service to them.

My anxieties increased and began to affect my health again. I prayed on, but the thought of all the ramifications and developments alarmed me more and more.

I had been a Christian long enough to have learnt that the problem of suffering offers one of the greatest challenges to a balanced and mature Christian faith.

For so many it seems to prove that life, far from being the expression of a God of love, is rather the product of blind chance, or worse—a merciless torture at the hands of some evil fiend.

But I had seen too much to believe that life was just a matter of chance, and I knew God too well in other ways to accept him as someone who would use suffering as a punishment.

But the suffering of sick children was something else again. My reading of the Bible had shown me some reasons why a God of love could allow suffering. Some of it was certainly a direct result of human selfishness, deceit, intolerance, and all the many evils mankind simply accepts. But so much suffering seemed unfair, undeserved, unreasonable. Why should it happen to this particular person—or to me?

Jesus' disciples struggled with this problem when they watched him curing a blind man. They asked Jesus whose sin had caused the disease—the man's or that of his parents. Jesus said simply: neither. This man's blindness was allowed so that God could be given the praise and glory when he was healed. But that did not answer *all* the questions. Certainly a miracle like that could show that God cared—a fact doubly underlined by the way in which his Son, Jesus, entered into our sufferings, enduring pain and death to spare us. But what about a little child who would never be healed? How were we to take that?

I was confused and challenged at the same time. But whatever my personal deliberations, the practical point remained: Nina or no Nina? Nicholas or no Nicholas? What were we—what was I—to do, back at the Coach House?

It seemed then that a useful, practical step would be to get hold of the children's doctor at the local hospital and find out for myself what provision had been made for handicapped children in the Stockport area. She might be able to tell me not only how many there were, but also what was done for them under the various National Health schemes. Then, at least, I would be in a better position to advise the mothers who came to me.

I wrote to the paediatrician at the hospital, asking her simply about the handicap situation. Perhaps, I thought, we could meet for a chat about what was on offer for disabled children and the like. She wrote back promptly and asked me to come to the hospital to see her.

So, very anxiously, I presented myself on the appointed day to this doctor at the hospital. I found her in a little alcove closed off from the busy main ward, wearing a regulation white coat and a mildly impatient frown. She was sipping a glass of milk.

She invited me to sit down and, taking a swift glance at her watch, quizzed me about my interest. I explained about Felicity, Nina and Nicholas—at which she nodded—and then repeated the questions I had penned in my letter to her. What was the handicap problem in Stockport—and what was the normal Local Authority or Health Service solution?

She took a sip of her milk and unloaded the facts.

She took on 500 new cases a year, of which 200 a year would probably remain with significant handicaps. There was no provision whatsoever in Stockport for this sort of child. There were a couple of nurseries relatively near—one in Manchester and one in Cheshire. The latter was for mentally handicapped children—and a few of her patients went there.

Otherwise all she had to offer was some physiotherapy at the hospital. Most children had about twenty minutes or so twice a week. She thought that there were then about 1,000 pre-school handicapped children in Stockport.

She paused and looked up at me with the tight smile of one who has a lot on her plate but who with relentless commitment is managing to see it through.

'And there we have it.'

She hadn't the slightest conception of the utter turmoil that these bare facts and figures had generated in my heart. Visions of hundreds of sightless, babbling children, hobbling and jerking around, crying out, falling down, helpless—with their desperate and exhausted mothers all trying to cope, filled my mind. Not only Nina and Nicholas and Felicity—but a thousand such. And all in need of expert care, time and attention, love and support.

And nothing, or virtually nothing, was being done. Good grief, even our half-hour chats with Nina and her mum over the gate were more than she was getting from the State! She had told me as much, but somehow I had not believed her. Not at the dawn of the progressive seventies, with Britain on the crest of an economic wave.

The doctor was speaking again.

'Mrs Wyatt, it seems to me that you are just the sort of person who can give time and care to these children. Why don't you start something to help? I could refer to you, say, a dozen to start with—and you see what you can do.'

My mouth dropped open but no sound came out. Here was I, asking her, for my own peace of mind, to confirm that I was doing the right thing in just thinking about accepting two severely handicapped children into my playgroup, and here she was, offering to give me twelve *more* just like that. Offering them, after three minutes' conversation, to an unqualified, mixed up, shaken and frightened person like me.

'Right, Mrs Wyatt, I'll be in touch.' She stood up abruptly, drinking the last of her milk as she rose. 'I'm sorry, but I have another appointment. Thank you for coming . . . you can see yourself out?'

I could—barely.

I fumbled my way back along the stark, clattering, hospital corridors, scarcely noticing where I was going. The warm sun struck down onto my bare head as I ducked out into the noisy grey streets and made it to the bus stop. I stood there, rocking with emotion. The street, the cars and the sun dissolved before my eyes in a flood of tears.

Whatever had I done?

Chapter Seven

FIRST STEPS

I returned from the hospital shocked and devastated by the doctor's comments. Not only were there apparently no facilities for the handicapped in the Stockport community but the doctor's offer of a 'dozen or so' handicapped children, coming as it did on top of my own crisis, had just about finished me.

What could I do? I turned, of course, to John for comfort and support, and we prayed about it together. I think that the act of prayer itself can be a great comforter and calmer of the shattered spirit. But I also know that God, by his Spirit, is more than just a comforter. He is an executive as well. Here I was confronted with the (to me) virtually unthinkable, and certainly unmanageable. I was in need of more than comfort and calm for my soul. I needed some action.

In a few days, if the doctor kept her word (though, surely, she couldn't mean it?) I would be getting details through my letter-box of handicapped children who would, in some measure, now be my direct concern. And there was also Nina and Nicholas to decide about. God simply had to come up with something. I knew he could. Look at the Coach House, or our own home for that matter.

As we prayed on I gradually felt a new sense of purpose. Somehow I became certain that God was saying to me: 'Yes, I want you to help these handicapped children, for my sake. Go forward and trust me.' The Bible says that faith is essentially 'being sure of what we hope for and certain of what we do not see'. I believed this and so, although I was still very disturbed by the implications, I went ahead in trust.

Even so, I did not just turn around and admit Nicholas and Nina. A word from God did not give me the instant ability or training to take care of handicapped children. Whatever risks the doctor was prepared to take with me, I was not the kind of person to take risks with other people's children without some sort of experience and formal skills to hand.

So I began to read and research. I read everything I could find about handicapped children. Further help came through the pages of *Child Education*, a magazine I was already taking regularly. It advertised a film and seminar to be led in London by a Dr Ron Faulkener—a general practitioner who had set up something called an 'opportunity group' in connection with handicapped children in a family case of his. I went to the London seminar and discovered the full story.

He had been doctor to a family with twin girls. One of them was a Down's Syndrome child, but all along he had encouraged the mother to treat the two children in the same way, although the 'normal' one was obviously much more capable than the other.

He was disconcerted to find, however, that when they both reached playschool age there was nowhere they could both attend together. As a consequence he had set up an 'opportunity group'—as he called it—

of his own. In doing this he had also found that there were a number of other local handicapped children who could benefit, along with their normal brothers and sisters, all learning to relate together in the playgroup environment. In addition he made a specific point of asking the mothers along. They too could benefit a great deal from the experience, he felt.

Shades of Felicity! It certainly gave me food for thought as I travelled home that night to Stockport. Perhaps, after all, bringing a handicapped child into a normal playgroup might be of actual *benefit* to the child, in terms of their treatment and therapy. Far from just amusing and taking care of them, it might even do them good! Strange though it might seem now, at the time I had not really considered the medical benefits that an active playgroup might have to offer to such children. I was looking at them (as so many automatically do) as a medical *problem* with which we would have to cope if the child were to participate in our activities.

But the facts of Charnwood remained. I was no doctor and was in no position to try experiments. I felt I could only continue my research and, once again, it was *Child Education* that gave me my next major opportunity.

It announced a week-long Easter seminar on 'pre-school handicapped children' to be run at Oxford under the auspices of the Spastic Society. A whole range of lectures and presentations were to be given. This was just what I wanted, so off I went, leaving my family at the mercy of John's cooking for a week— but on a very virtuous excuse: my concern for handicapped children! It was infinitely worthwhile. I met with the very cream of informed society on the subject. I lapped up the lectures from doctors and educationalists and psychologists—and my horizons opened wide. Great strides were being made in meeting the medical needs of young handicapped children of all kinds. Therapies were being developed, equipment invented and insights gained on all fronts—except, I noted, when it came to teaching them to be *people* in the community.

Most of the children discussed were attending—and had been under observation in—special schools where, from a very early age, they certainly were receiving good educational instruction. But the schools were segregated institutions, often quite a distance from the children's homes. Inevitably, it seemed to me, the long journeys involved and the isolation of the schools separated the children from their families, friends and community. Consequently by the time they were ready to leave school and take their place in the world, they lacked even the basic social skills and experiences needed to achieve such simple things as making friends, talking to employers or just generally relating.

Conversely, it also seemed evident, even from my own limited observations, that normal children were having so little experience of getting to know those with handicaps that, when they did finally meet, there was instant embarrassment and unthinking rejection. The very presence of hearing aids, or calipers or—worse still—a wheelchair, clearly showed their users to be different and therefore most likely difficult.

Yes, in Oxford there certainly were a great many important thoughts and discoveries flying about, but very little in areas I instinctively felt to be equally vital. For, even if new discoveries cured a great many handicaps, what shape would the ex-patient be in to take on 'normal life' afterwards?

I returned from Oxford excited and challenged. I had become convinced that somehow at Charnwood we did have a responsibility to find a way of allowing the handicapped children we had met to mix in and play with our ordinary playgroup children. Their mothers were instinctively right—the children needed that experience, no matter what their disability.

This was, for me, a significant conclusion. But it needed more than this to get something going. It needed experience. It needed action. I felt that I had done what I could. What I wanted now was some action from God's side.

It was at about this stage in the proceedings that the hospital doctor began to fulfil her word. Letters from the hospital began to arrive at my home. And, after opening one or two, if I hadn't been prepared for this by my recent studies I would have arranged to leave the neighbourhood overnight with no forwarding address. As it was, I soon learned to have my breakfast some time before I read the letters and to be safely seated in a supportive chair. The information was so disturbing it completely shook me—and totally removed my appetite.

The stories were horrific.

One was so extreme, so ridiculous, that I determined to call the doctor's bluff and investigate it myself.

'Dear Mrs Wyatt,' ran the letter. 'I thought you might be interested in Sharon. She is aged two-and-a-half and blind. Her mother is a hemiplegic (that meant she was partially paralysed down one side). She married at sixteen and bore Sharon at seventeen.

Last year she lost a baby and is now pregnant again, though we think there will be complications with the birth. She is now nineteen. Her husband is unemployed. Perhaps,' she concluded, 'Sharon is one of the children you would consider helping?'

Quite apart from the incredible nature of the story, what really stung me was the consultant's hope that I already had the resources to help this poor little girl.

Surely there was no one in Stockport with problems like these? Moss Side perhaps, or inner London—but here? Never. I borrowed John's car and set off.

I drove slowly down the poorer streets of the town and found the address—a small terraced house in a very run-down area. I knocked on the door.

After some time and much banging and clattering it opened, and there stood a woman who looked over forty, with a blind child on one arm. The other arm hung uselessly by her side. As she stood there, I could see that her whole weight was on one leg. And she was pregnant.

'Yeah?' she enquired.

I stood there. I had nothing to say. I had been so certain that this situation didn't exist that I had prepared nothing. Desperately I searched round for something to say, and then I remembered the girl's name. I quickly introduced myself and enquired after 'little Sharon', explaining with a rush that I was thinking of starting some sort of group locally and had come to see if she was, well, interested?

But she could offer nothing intelligible for my enlightenment, either concerning her interest in a group, or on the subject of Sharon's health. After a few moments I fled, muttering my excuses.

This was terrible. There obviously was this sort of

disadvantaged person here in Stockport. I could not believe it. But I had to—I had seen it in the flesh. I knew I had to do something to help Sharon—and her mum. I was concerned, really concerned now. But without the skill . . ?

It was a bright morning in spring. The blossom on the apple trees was swirling, foamy and white, on the twigs and branches, sending a snowy shower down onto several delighted upturned faces playing in the garden, when yet another mother turned up at the Coach House gate to put her child down on the long waiting-list.

Her name was Anne. She was new to the district and quickly understood that, unfortunately, we couldn't fit her son in right away—not for many months in fact. But, instead of heading off immediately, she stopped a moment to play along with the children. She was obviously at home in the playgroup. Was she a nursery teacher? I wondered.

'Well, I am, actually, but not of your sort of children . . . I'm really used to teaching blind children.'

'Oh, *blind* children . . ?' I replied, feathers tickling up and down my spine.

'Oh, yes, I used to work at the Sunshine Nursery for Blind Children. I was so sorry to give it up when my husband's work brought him here. You don't happen to know of any blind children around here, do you? I would love to work with them again.'

I had to admit I knew of at least two.

'Oh, then you have them here?' she asked excitedly.

I explained my present state of hesitancy. She was not discouraged.

'But you could . . . you could have them here. I could help. I've got lots of time now. We could find the time, surely. In the afternoons, maybe?'

I thought of my home, my husband, my four children, my work at church, my . . .

'I suppose we could.'

But I made her wait. I wanted more help. If God could bring her along, he could bring others too.

Anne got busy. She made a few enquiries among the other mothers who brought children in the mornings (the only time we operated, then). There already was, she discovered, a mother who had trained as a children's ward sister in an orthopaedic hospital, another who was a nursery nurse, a health visitor, a physiotherapist . . .

One by one these skilled professionals came to me to offer their services in the event of my deciding to start a special group—just in case I had been thinking along those lines at all.

I was beginning to feel got at. Caution: God at work!

They all mentioned, too, that they wanted their own children to come along with them— partly, of course, because they could hardly leave them on their own at home but also because they thought that the 'mix' would be a very important experience for them. Dr Faulkener's findings exactly. We should listen to mothers' thoughts so much more!

I felt rather ashamed at their obvious enthusiasm, compared to my own doubts and fears. It was evident God was making the arrangements—using people as part of his plan, arranging the bringing together, the timing and the prompting.

The way ahead was clear—my unofficial pact with God had been honoured.

I drew up a rota of staff for one (Wednesday) afternoon a week starting with eight normal and eight handicapped children. In it I included little Sharon, Nina and Nicholas, plus five others from the doctor's list. We, too, would call it an 'opportunity group', and we would do our level best to encourage those with handicaps to develop what abilities they could, in the context of 'normal' play with all the other children. Also, we were very clear about wanting all their mothers to join in too—to learn to live and play with their own disadvantaged sons and daughters, to meet one another (somewhere other than in a waiting-room) and to find hope instead of despair in being the mother of a handicapped child. It may not seem such a great step. But it was. For no longer could we call ourselves just a playgroup. With God's help we had become (and the words are still written over the door): 'Charnwood—for normal *and* handicapped children.'

Chapter Eight

NINA

We started on the first Wednesday afternoon in June. I remember it because I had an entirely sleepless night the night before. Would the mums be happy to come? Would we be able to cope? And so on. I had sent invitations out. But that in itself didn't mean too much. Well, we would soon see.

I took upon myself the task of getting little Sharon and her mother to the group, summarily informing John that I would need the car that afternoon and every Wednesday for the foreseeable future. Unprotesting, he took the bus to work.

I went round to the dingy house, only to find that Sharon's mum wasn't quite ready to go out. She wasn't ready at all. She obviously hadn't really expected me to come. But I stood firmly by the door while she limped around to make Sharon a bottle, pack a spare nappy, fetch her coat, etc. Eventually I got her out to the car and off we went.

As we drew up at the Coach House—pretty late—I saw, to my intense relief, that the group was in full swing. The mums were naturally rather reserved in the strange new situation but the children were having a whale of a time, with happy gurgles and giggles coming from all quarters.

Going in, I noticed for the first time something that is now always remarked on by visitors to present-day Charnwood. *At a quick glance it was a job to tell the handicapped from the normal.*

Taking a second look some of them were still difficult to pick out—even those with multiple handicap problems. They were all just children. It was a revealing insight and many of my fears evaporated in a moment. I found I was looking at the child first (as I always used to as a teacher) and not the handicap.

Over there was Nicholas, learning about cars again by being carefully pushed along in one—though he was rather frustrated by a deaf boy who had decided to waylay him by lying down in front of the car, much to his own entertainment.

A Down's Syndrome girl was tackling some complicated-looking building blocks with one of the helpers, and a girl prone to epileptic fits was being shown round the playhouse by a very house-proud little boy whose only fault was a certain amount of childish pomposity. She, wisely, was suitably impressed.

Anne was sitting down right in the middle of all this activity, bouncing blind little Nina on her knees and tickling her. But this was not just messing around. By her actions she was telling Nina that there were lots of good experiences to be had 'out here'— and that to be bounced and tickled was one of the very nicest. In fact, over the next few weeks Anne learned quite a lot about apparently deaf, dumb and blind Nina. She quickly found out that Nina understood simple speech, so hearing was no real problem after all—rather the reverse. Because she did not move and could not speak she was finding the noise in some of the sessions rather confusing and alarming, though she seemed, still, to be very unresponsive.

Then one day, in a quiet corner, Anne discovered that if she spoke *about* Nina rather than *to* her she attracted the child's attention—and clear response— out of natural curiosity, Nina being unaware that anyone was watching her.

'Look, Grace, this is a funny little girl. I think she's got a ribbon on her hair,' Anne said pointedly to me. We watched without a word as the little fingers groped up to find the ribbon and then stopped.

Anne continued: 'And I think she's also got a bracelet up her sleeve.' We watched, excited, as the little fingers once again searched until the bracelet was located, and then stayed there. Her head was to one side, her lips parted—all was attention, waiting to comprehend the next words.

'Now show us your tummy, Nina,' said Anne. Immediately the lips closed and the sightless face grew slack and indifferent; the fingers dropped away.

What a self-conscious little girl we had just discovered! As the sessions went on we managed to gain her confidence, enough for her to respond directly to us, and it was evident that she understood a great deal. She soon learned to recognize our voices but was never quite relaxed until she had sat on our knees and frisked us over first, running her fingers lightly over our hair and faces, and our bust—this was most important. She soon learnt who was well-endowed and who wasn't—matching sound to shape like the sharpest chorus line director! In fact, that wasn't so wide of the mark, for we also discovered early on that music was deeply significant to Nina. After a while, when I was at the piano, she would sit on my knee, place her hands over mine and rock gently to the rhythm of whatever nursery rhyme I was playing and singing. Then, if I stopped suddenly, she would continue to hum the melody perfectly on the note, finishing with a giggle of pleasure. She learned new songs with ease and could soon hum every one we used in the nursery.

What was more, *she began to use the songs to communicate with us*.

Somehow she deduced that, if she deliberately hummed certain phrases from the nursery rhymes, we would work out the words and then could (usually) guess what it was she wanted.

'Where do you want to play now, Nina?'

'Hum, hum . . . Goosey Goosey Gander . . . where shall I wander . . ? UPSTAIRS (big hummmm), downstairs and in my lady's chamber!' With the emphasis on the big hum 'upstairs', we weren't left in too much doubt as to the next place for playing.

Mind you, it rather depended on the rhyme. 'See-saw Marjory Daw' and 'Mary Mary Quite Contrary, how-does-your-garden-grow', weren't too bad for swings and garden but when it came to 'Humpty Dumpty' (Sit on the wall? Play horses? A story about kings and queens?), or 'Ba, Ba Black Sheep' (Cuddly toy? Take her jersey off? Play with a boy?), things could get a little strained unless we caught the emphasis just right. Fortunately Nina was good-humoured and if we got it wrong she would just laugh scornfully and start all over again.

In fact she became my regular companion at the piano for the sing-song and 'band' sessions, though one day one little boy asked me what she was doing up there holding my hands.

I told him: 'She can't see because she hasn't any eyes, so she uses my hands instead to find things out.'

He promptly sat himself down at a nearby table and said: 'Put her on my knee now and let her use my hands—she can have my fingers instead of her eyes!'

But I wanted her to talk. I was sure she could—she just had to be encouraged to get round to it. She was three years old and as well as being blind she had severe cerebral palsy. But my ignorance at that time of what this meant was my strength. I didn't know the odds. Anne was pleased with her progress so far but I wasn't going to let up until we had some words. To a mum, words are pretty well the most important thing in the world, and I just knew that Nina was up to it.

I latched onto the work of some experienced American music therapists—Nordorf and Robbins— and, remembering Nina's well-developed musical ability, thought this might be the avenue to verbal communication. Their method of therapy was to write a song, with actions, specifically centred on the child they were trying to help. This often captured the child's interest and attention enough for them to teach some linked skill.

I decided to give it a try. So I sat down, got out my pen, and began writing, like Rogers and Hart, though with more precision.

The song went something like this:

'Nina, she's got two hands,
Mrs Wyatt, she's got two hands,
Everybody else has got two hands,
How many hands have we got?
TWO-O-O!'

As you can see, it certainly takes the wind out of *42nd Street*. That's what comes of being a musical family!

After I had sung this through a couple of times Nina showed her appreciation by a giggle. We then brought on our 'choir'—everyone else who wanted to join in—and we all went through it again, shouting out the answer at appropriate moments and waving or feeling our hands. Nina joined in with the melody—humming, of course—and grabbed at my hands as I did hers. We repeated this performance over the next few music sessions until one day, when everyone else was becoming so thoroughly bored with this repetitive song, they were slow in coming in with the TWO! Not so Nina, who opened up with a perfectly formed 'OO'. We had broken the sound barrier!

We all clapped heartily and demanded—and got—a repeat performance. Nina had started to articulate. What a day! Later, thinking about it, I realized that by using the song in the way I had (not entirely as Messrs Nordoff and Robbins had intended), I had stumbled on one of the keys to success in teaching handicapped children: motivation.

We knew that with Nina's particular disability it required a disproportionate amount of effort to control her tongue, lips and breathing to produce the controlled sounds of speech. Our problem had been to get her to *want* to, enough to give it that extra go. It was not so much the music that had helped Nina, it was her desire to finish the song properly for the others. Her wish had forced her to make that additional effort.

I could see that the sort of incentives that stimulated a normal child's development were equally appropriate for children like Nina. No formalized one-to-one therapy could have produced this result.

So often since then we have noticed how the eagerness of a handicapped child to participate in, and contribute to, some shared activity serves as the driving force enabling him or her to master a vital skill.

We deprive children of this simple, but powerful, motivation if we segregate them. It may be very hard to learn to hold your head up straight to please your therapist, but it is no trouble at all if the effort is needed to help you see where to plant the winning domino at the end of a fiercely fought game!

So, gradually, Nina learned to speak—vowel sounds first, then consonants, and eventually recognizable words. Not only did the other children encourage her with their interest but we also learned to 'reward' her with her great love: music.

After each time of special learning—speech, hand control, shape appreciation, whatever it was—when it was over she would slip down from her chair and crawl over slowly, by sense and touch, to where she knew the piano stood. Getting to the stool she would hold on to it and pull herself up—then quietly hum the song she wished us to play. She always got her choice. There was a smile of achievement and delight on her lips and sightless features that none of us could refuse.

In many ways it was the very least we could do for such a brave and lovable little girl. For into her closed, shuttered and damaged life she had helped us to bring light—not the light of sight, for without eyes that was impossible—but the light of understanding, of communication, of pleasure and fun, a childlike wonder at the beauty of music and of friendship, a gritty response to challenge, and true delight at achievement. So much, for one little girl. How small we often felt when we realized what God had enabled us to do!

Of course Nina was not the only child to respond to the stimulation of the playgroup. The new toys, the activity, the noise and excitement, provoked nearly all the children to exceed the expectations of their parents—under the careful control of the experienced women who had volunteered to help.

And it wasn't just the children who showed signs of benefiting. The mothers too began to be affected by the group. Quiet and unsure though they may have been on the first day—they soon fell into the routine and began to look forward to Wednesdays with an unexpected sense of anticipation.

Sharon's mother was, of course, the one I noticed most, since it was still my self-appointed duty to pick the two of them up. One afternoon in late summer, I drew up outside her home. She greeted me at the door right away, indicating that she was ready to leave immediately. Although by now heavily pregnant, she wore what appeared to me to be a brand new maternity gown. Her hair, which had straggled mousily round her shoulders, was now a resplendent copper hue and back-combed up into a rigidly lacquered beehive. (Sharon, too, had on a new outfit.) We went straight out to the car and, as she sat down in the passenger seat, I could see she was sporting a magnificent set of false eyelashes.

I was just about to compliment her on her appearance and ask where they were going afterwards when my brain engaged, along with the clutch, and I shut up promptly. Of course, she wasn't going on anywhere afterwards. This was it. This was for going out to Charnwood. Because of the opportunity group, to her normal social round of hospital waiting-room, supermarket and laundrette had been added a completely new range of friends and experiences—plus something, in common, to talk about. This modest afternoon was the high spot of the week.

I was amazed. All we had to offer was a run-down old Coach House with hard benches and bare floors. It was a poor setting for the making of friendships and the discussing of fears and problems together. Yet I could see, when I looked at it, that Charnwood had become an eagerly anticipated social venue for the mothers who met there. A warmth of welcome and companionship had been generated.

It was apparent to me that the pain of being the mother of a handicapped child was often unbearably increased by a sense of isolation, guilt and of 'being different'. Bringing the mothers together with their children had helped them, too. Shared experiences eased the grief and brought hope.

At last they were not alone, and that was very good.

Chapter Nine

A MEETING-PLACE

As I drove Sharon's mother to the group that summer afternoon I determined to try to pursue an idea I had had for a place where these mothers could meet on their own during the session—somewhere near to the group, but separate from it, and available during the session. Not all the time, of course, for the mothers needed to play constructively with their children, with a helper's guidance. But a little meeting-place to return to later would give them the chance for a moment of release from the tension of coping, for them to relax over a coffee, to socialize and chat, to set down for a short while the horrible weight of responsibility that had so suddenly settled on them—a place where they could be girls. Sharon's mother was only nineteen! Many were about that age—and disadvantaged, some coming from broken homes, wrecked marriages, living as professional or personal failures, even before the handicapped child came into their lives.

Surely there must be someone living nearby who could offer their front room for an hour once a week? It would have to be close by. I prayed about it, but nothing happened. I was nonplussed. I had made it a personal rule by this time that I would not move ahead on anything to do with Charnwood without seeing God take the lead. With the help he had given us so far, that wasn't unreasonable! So I waited. The idea was good, it was important; now what would happen?

Nothing. So I broke my rule. If God was not going to help, I would have a go myself. Something must be done.

So I went ahead and approached one of the mums who lived only a few doors down from us. Her place would do nicely. She seemed a helpful, kindly sort—surely she would be able to have a few mums in to chat together?

The whole thing was a disaster. Talk about a cold response: it was icy. Her husband, she said, would be concerned about the furniture. She certainly wouldn't consider the idea. Not at all. In fact she was surprised I had asked. I retired, very hurt.

'I'm sorry,' I said to God in repentance. 'It seems you don't feel there is a need here after all.'

We closed at the end of the summer term with no meeting-place, although the group as a whole had been a real success. The progress of certain of the children—Nina for one—had been magnificent and we could not think of a single child who had not developed in some way.

A few days into the holidays a lady turned up on my doorstep at home. She had a child slightly above playgroup age but wondered if for a term or two he might come along to the playgroup before he went on to school. I thought we could help. After term began she quickly heard about the 'opportunity group'. Were there any vacancies for mothers to help? She had had experience with playgroups and family work. I had to say I was sorry but we were oversubscribed with professional volunteers already.

'Well, if there is anything I can do . . .' she said, as she left. I looked down at her address. Clifton Road. She would be the closest mum to us at the Coach House. But I'd had my fingers burnt once. I was saying nothing.

The autumn term proceeded and the weather was frightful. Wednesday after Wednesday the rain lashed down on the windows of the building and the wind beat about our Edwardian eaves. People on the radio were saying that it was the worst autumn for fifty years. I could believe it. Although the children were again playing happily, the mums could not even pop outside for a smoke or a walk to get a break. Most of the time they felt cooped up and fretful.

After one particularly vicious afternoon I came home feeling a little depressed and found myself praying—and I suddenly remembered the mother in Clifton Road!

Should I call her? Yes, I would. It had been a horrible afternoon.

She answered the phone and, hearing who was calling, said immediately:

'Oh, good. Are you going to ask me to help?'

'Well, yes, as a matter of fact I was.'

'Now, before you go on, Mrs Wyatt, the thing I've been thinking about is perhaps to get those mothers away somewhere for a little while. I live very close—it would be no trouble at all for them to come round to me for a cup of tea and a chat . . . I'm used to this anyway, as I'm training to be a counsellor, so maybe I could help some of them as well.'

So the mothers began to meet together in her comfortable lounge and Ann was able to share their conversation and even advise them if they wanted.

As the group expanded we came across some horrific family situations—often on top of the problems of dealing with a handicapped child. There were mothers living alone, deserted by their men, or shunned and blamed by the family for bearing a handicapped child. Two of the mothers had attempted suicide and all of them, without exception, were depressed and on tranquillizers. Fellowship and counsel were vital. Just to know there were others who could not cope with screaming children—even 'normal' children—was a tremendous thing. Someone else understood. That was healing on its own.

As the 'opportunity group' began to expand and take up other afternoons, we sometimes asked some of the mothers and children to come back more frequently—for the sake of the mother as much as the child.

Although Ann was now giving special counsel, our concern for the mothers and families of children at the playgroup had been a quiet aspect of Charnwood from the very beginning, even before I had become aware of and concerned for handicapped children. We followed through—and were often caught up in—many family problems simply as a consequence of taking the children into the playgroup.

In our increasingly unstable society the modern inclination for 'open', go-where-you-please relationships leaves behind a truly frightening trail of disorientated children and broken relationships. But few want to see this, to know that children are left hurt, damaged, destroyed, by something as simple as infidelity or marital deceit.

At the playgroup we cannot avoid listening to the children's talk. They say what goes on at home, they

October 1977: Cliff Richard, Charnwood's patron, plays the tambourine with Jane, who has Down's Syndrome (see chapter thirteen).

A group of children enjoy a ride in the go-cart specially made for Charnwood by engineering apprentices. In front is Jacob (see page 117) Grace Wyatt is at the back.

The Mayor of Stockport helps Nicholas cut the tape at the official opening of Charnwood's new headquarters (see page 143 and chapter six). Standing are Nicholas's father and the principal of Charnwood, Grace Wyatt.

Charnwood's present building was opened in October 1979. Today 170 children come to the Centre each week. Fifty of these are handicapped.

The Prairie, which ferries children and parents to and from the Centre, was donated by the Llankelly Foundation.

Alexander, who has cerebral palsy, finds it better to play across his mother's knee. He is fitting car shapes into a board, watched by Paul.

Effie has Möbius Syndrome and is very shy. She is learning to touch and feel, and making friends at the same time.

This bucking bronco is quite safe to ride! But Sarah, a volunteer helper, is watching in case Alex needs her.

James, who is profoundly deaf, loves to make things. Here he shows
Grace his garden.

Paul controls the lights in a special playhouse made by Alexander's grandad.

Everyone enjoys the sand-pit. It's better without shoes, but best of all to sit in.

Dough is always a favourite. In 1982, when this photograph was taken, no one thought that Jacob (right: see page 117) would ever walk.

1985—and Jacob is walking!

After a hectic day, it's good to know that there will be a ride home.

Claire walks for the first time, helped by her mother, Pat (right) and Ann, a volunteer.

Many very special children have passed through Charnwood in the years since it began. One of them was Robert, seated here on his mother's knee (see Postscript).

say what is happening. Long before the parent gives an inkling—if they ever do—that anything might be wrong, we know what their home is like, what pressures are there. And we can see the effect on the child. Sometimes we feel as though we have been called to serve on a domestic battlefield, as nurses or doctors tending the wounded—finding that many of them, shockingly, are children. Our next generation . . !

And not all of this comes from the uneducated, the illiterate, the uninformed. We have had doctors, professors, soldiers, accountants—of both sexes—shouting, screaming and crying about their lives, their children or their partners in the playgroup office, or at our home. An education, to whatever level, is no passport to stability or wisdom when it comes to the family.

Occasionally these outbursts have led to a sharing of my own Christian convictions. And so through painful encounters God has entered some adult lives, and changed them for the better, through the work of Charnwood. I have seen him save an ugly situation from becoming a disaster—for people from a wide variety of lifestyles.

Our beliefs are our own and, daily, at Charnwood, I work alongside many who profess to none. But if there is a problem and I am asked for advice (something that happens, now, almost daily), my answer must be based on my own experience of a God who loves and promises to help all who recognize their need. But of course being seen as a 'do-gooder' is not always the best thing, even if you do manage to do some good. Many refuse to believe you have anything to offer except sentimentality.

This was impressed on me most vividly—indeed it had a profound effect on the future of Charnwood—when we received a visit from the local Medical Officer of Health. He was a Scottish doctor with a rigid old-style training and background.

He marched into the Coach House one day shortly after the handicapped children joined us. Nina was by now coming to some of the morning groups, being so quick on the uptake. He was appalled and outraged. He took one look round, taking in Nina who was in my arms, and the fairly basic facilities.

'Ye really are an evil woman, bringing yon wee bairn here!' he thundered. 'It's nae more than a garret!'

The whole happy group came to a trembling halt.

'I'm goin' to close ye doon if it's the last thing I do!' he exclaimed.

I tried to intervene and explain that the 'wee bairn' was now very frightened and offended—since she was very perceptive—and that the other children were none too secure now either.

He was unconcerned. Medical problems required medical answers. Feelings, particularly children's feelings, didn't come into it.

'What do ye know about the bairn? Stupid, sentimental women like you are a menace!' he shouted.

By this time I was in tears and Nina was shaking with fear.

'Look, please go,' I pleaded.

'I'll gae,' he confirmed, 'but I'll finish ye. I'll finish ye for guid!'

I sat down, weakly. He looked round grimly for his hat. It was nowhere to be found.

'Woman, wheere's ma haat?' he demanded.

Distracted, I confessed I didn't know what he had

done with it. He rushed round the building, but could find no hat. Meanwhile I had the strange feeling that the chair I was sitting on was, how shall I put it, a little more contoured than usual. A subdued choking from one of the helpers served to confirm my suspicions. I was sitting on it.

The doctor roared back in: 'Nae haat!'

Silently I got up, bent down and retrieved the now depressed headgear. There was a moment of electric tension—a forbidding glare. Then he turned on his heel and left without another word. I never saw him again.

He couldn't close us down, for we were properly qualified and operating legally in all that we were doing. But, as a consequence of his report to the Council, from then on we could interest no one professionally in what we were doing—either with the normal or the handicapped children. I wrote to the Director of Education, to ask for expert psychological help (it was available) but received no reply. The doctor at the hospital was advised to send us no more details of handicapped children. Charnwood had been officially blacklisted.

From then on nothing good could be said or heard about us officially for, once the report was made, the authorities would see only what they expected to see. We were branded for life—or so we thought.

It was a very depressing, jarring note in the early life of a scheme which had actually turned out most successfully in terms of helping the mothers and their handicapped children to make something of life. Whatever the criticisms—and we knew we weren't perfect—we had made a proper start as best we knew how. I badly needed experienced long-term advice

and help, and had been hoping that the local
Education and Health Authorities might enable me
to gain it. As an ordinary nursery teacher I needed to
discover much more about the whole world of
children with handicaps. One week in Oxford was
not enough. Now my only apparent resource—my
access to the local end of the 'system'—had given me
the cold shoulder. But, in the event, help came from
a most unexpected quarter—and it has been coming
ever since.

I had noticed that one of the children in the
morning playgroup wasn't learning to speak
properly. In fact he never ever spoke. He was over
three years old but he wouldn't say a thing. Yet from
the way he was playing I could see he was highly
intelligent. He just wouldn't spcak. His parents refused to believe that there was anything wrong with
the child. But I wasn't happy.

I contacted the wife of a friend who was a speech
therapist. She came along one morning and put the
boy through his paces.

'He has a major language disorder,' was her ver-
dict. I nerved myself to confront his parents. To ease
the situation the speech therapist suggested I
mention to the parents that their little boy was *so*
bright that the Department of Audiology at Manchester University—a major hearing and speech research unit—would be interested to see him.

She was right. The Audiology Department did
want to know and the parents were sufficiently impressed to overcome their annoyance at my interference. One of the team—Betty Byers-Brown—
later got in touch with me, explaining that she hoped
the boy would soon be talking (which he was) but that
he was fortunate that his condition had been spotted

in the nick of time. She wondered how I had come to notice him. Was I in touch with others like him?

So I invited her round to see the Coach House, in all its rather tattered glory.

She was amazed.

'This is fantastic,' she chortled. 'Do you have any idea of the value of the work you are doing here? I've never seen anything like it. You are really pioneering integrated education!'

I was pleased she liked it, not too many people had. I wasn't quite sure what integrated education was but I knew we were in the frontline of something, that was for sure!

She immediately asked if she could send some of her students along to see the work—and perhaps learn something of the interaction between handicapped and normal children. They would be degree students, who could really benefit from watching my 'research', but if I didn't mind . . .

So we came to an understanding, which has certainly proved priceless to me over the years—and I trust invaluable for her and her department, too. I would call her up if I wanted to know something more about a particular handicap (she had much more than just speech and hearing information at her disposal), or to read a paper, talk to a psychologist, put a query about a child or whatever. And in return I would take her students for practical 'frontline' experience.

Although not as embracing or 'accepting' as the community support which I had so hoped for, this has proved a lifeline time and time again.

If we were now moving out into the larger world, it was becoming apparent that Charnwood must too.

The lease from the dentist was up, having run now for eight years. The buildings were tatty (there was some truth in the jibe about 'yon garret') and I felt we needed to establish ourselves more formally to be effective, perhaps as a registered charity.

We knew what our work meant to those who came, and the university link had confirmed its value, whatever anyone else had said. Maybe if we could somehow find 'purpose-built' accommodation we would be accepted along with other servants of the community.

So, once again, I started to hunt for new premises.

Chapter Ten

OPPOSITION

Everything now seemed to be coming at once: the idea of forming a charity, the need to move, and the increasing involvement with the educational and research aspects of handicapped children.

So, while I concerned myself about the move—the simple task of looking for a new roof to put over our heads—John focussed his attention on the formation of a Charitable Trust. One of the concrete promptings for this was that we were already receiving gifts 'for the work' and had no proper way to deal with them. Another was the need for formal recognition as an organization. We were already considered part of the Pre-school Playgroup Movement—which had accepted us and had now established as part of its own philosophy the 'opportunity group' idea.

Of course I intended going on with what I was doing in any case—I could see the value of the results. But we needed in the end to feel that we were not just cranks. I needed to! So we invited three friends, a headmistress of a county girls' school, a partner in a firm of accountants, and Ann of the 'mother's lounge', to join John as four trustees and made an application to the Charity Commissioners. Soon we hoped we would be known as the

Charnwood Trust.

At around the same time, quite independently of my search for new premises, a local property developer approached us with the offer of free access to a void piece of land—a plot otherwise totally enclosed by other property—in St Paul's Road, Heaton Moor. He said that if we could buy the land he would give us the vehicle access.

We had no money and the land would cost many thousands of pounds. But we went to have a look. We were surprised. The area was a place John knew well. Some years before, he had gone out for an early morning walk and had crossed this land by the narrow footpath to some fields (now developed housing) and had been moved to pause, as he looked out from this rising ground across Stockport to the grey roofs of distant Manchester, and pray.

His heart had gone out to all the people who would be making homes in the bright new houses springing up across this once green countryside between Stockport and the metropolis. Who would care for them spiritually? Who would share with them the message of Christ's love? He still remembered how he had felt in that place, and his return home that morning with the strong feeling that God had a work to do there. There was something in mind. Now, naturally, he was excited to think that God seemed to be leading us back to the same place.

We were advised to commission an architect to draw up plans for the sort of nursery we would ideally want—just to see if the Local Authority would grant planning permission. There was no point in even contemplating buying anything if we couldn't build on it when we had got it. So we did.

In a sense we were a bit like children planning a

fairy castle when it came to the design. Since there was no money we didn't have a budget to work to—so we simply went ahead and put in all the various things we knew would be really useful. We needed space—twenty-five square feet—for each child, and an area for indoor/outdoor play, a parents' room, toy library, toilets, safety stairs, special rooms for individual therapy. The list was pretty long, with me putting in odd extras as they came to mind. Why worry? This wasn't for real; it was just to test the temperature of the water, as it were. If we ever started talking seriously about building then things might be different, but at the moment we could dream all we wanted. The plans were drawn up and sent off to 'Planning' for Council approval. Meanwhile the Charity Commissioners had considered our case, approved our trustees and our work, and granted us charitable status. I was very relieved. Surely this would help us now in our search for a new building? Plans and land were an exciting prospect, but they were unrealistic with nothing in the bank. The plain facts were, we needed another building, already existing, to move into right now.

In October 1973 we held our first trustees meeting as the Charnwood Trust. Although ordinary as meetings go, it was an historic occasion for us. I was voted the grand salary of £45 per month for my services as 'Principal'.

But the year moved swiftly to its conclusion with the old Coach House becoming obviously more and more unsuitable for the work: the dry rot increased apace and the landlord was becoming impatient.

One cold Wednesday afternoon in December, after a difficult session with the children, I impulsively telephoned the Director of Education at the

Town Hall. I was feeling desperate. We were now a registered charity—I surely could raise some interest with someone? To my great surprise I was put through direct. Of course, I had prepared nothing to say.

But my mind sped along just ahead of my tongue as I introduced myself and explained that, as he had been unable to visit us, I had decided that he, the Director, could look forward to a visit at the Town Hall from the whole playgroup—handicapped children included—the following Monday.

I have no idea why I felt I should say that, or even suggest it. I didn't even know if any of the mums and children would be able to come, let alone all of them. But it seemed a good idea at the time. The Director was alarmed. Visions of the grave and clinical bureaucracy of the Town Hall being disturbed by invading hoards of pre-school youngsters—all coming just to see him—obviously didn't bear thinking about. He countered by offering to visit us instead.

'You're most kind,' I continued. 'I know you are a very busy man. You do know where to come?' I concluded sweetly. He assured me that he did.

To my surprise, the next Monday he actually turned up. And I had had time over the weekend to make some special arrangements for his reception. All the mums and children were there. The afternoon opportunity group mixed in with the morning playgroup. I wasn't being dishonest—I had suggested he see *all* the children and that is what he had accepted.

He came in and I began to introduce him to the mothers and helpers, and to some of the children. It wasn't long before I noticed a pallor creeping across his previously robust features. After seeing one particularly badly handicapped little boy I noticed that he was only nodding in reply to my continuous stream of information about the children. I took the hint and cut the tour short, leading him out into the fresh air.

He gulped in great draughts of the piercing frosty blast that whipped at the bare apple trees in the deserted garden.

'I had no idea,' he muttered. 'I really had no idea.' The colour returned slowly to his features. 'I can see that something must be done—you must find somewhere else.' His face brightened. 'And I know just the place,' he went on. 'There's a house in Mauldeth Road that belongs to the Authority—you can lease that, if it is suitable.'

Just like that! I was staggered. 'Well, thank you, God!' I sang in my heart. What an amazing answer to all our prayers (assuming the house was big enough and in reasonable shape, of course).

He promised to return with the Director of Social Services and the key, forthwith. And he was as good as his word. Back they came and we went to look round a lovely big mock Tudor detached house in Mauldeth Road.

The place exceeded my expectations. It was in good decorative order, it was dry, nearly an acre of garden stretched away to the rear, with a lovely pond—and Mauldeth Road was only a stone's throw from our present site at the Coach House (well, perhaps a little more, but certainly within convenient pram-pushing distance).

It was perfect. We left in the best of spirits, promising to be in touch about all the arrangements to be made for a short-term lease between the new Charnwood Trust and the helpful and understanding Local Authority.

But nothing happened. Christmas came and went, so did January and February, then March—and still nothing was heard from the Town Hall. Letters went unanswered. Neither director would talk to me on the phone. I was stonewalled. The Trust was stonewalled. Completely.

Then, just after Easter, we heard. The lease could not be approved because the Borough Council did not want the house used 'for private education'. This despite the fact that the handicapped children, their mothers, the helpers and their children, came to Charnwood free. Still, that was the stated reason. I discovered much later that, despite the two directors' collective support, all the others on the Council had apparently remembered the Scots doctor's disparaging report and had stamped us as wholly undesirable and therefore undeserving. Private education did not really come into it.

Our hopes were dashed.

The house in Mauldeth Road continued to stand empty, mocking me as I drove past it daily to the Coach House; and over the next few months of the summer I watched helplessly as it became the target for vandals. Windows were smashed, tiles ripped off, lead stolen, toilets and fittings were ripped out or broken, the garden let go. The pond became a rubbish dump.

By autumn my 'special provision' from God was little more than a boarded-up derelict. In addition, all our planning applications were being refused. We re-submitted and re-submitted, the architect re-designing to the specifications that had apparently, been the cause of the refusal. But always something else was pointed out for change—and back came the plans.

One night I had a phone call.

'Mrs Wyatt, this is an anonymous phone call from a member of the planning team in Stockport Borough Council.'

'Oh, yes,' I said, as though this sort of thing happened every evening. 'What can I do for you?'

The man quietly explained that we would never get approval for our plans (or indeed anything else), no matter how often we re-applied. We were considered undesirable and effectively blacklisted—and that was that. He felt personally, however, that we were needed in Stockport and that this was patently unfair. If we were to let it be known around the Town Hall that we were preparing to appeal to the Minister in London over the issue, he felt things might change quite considerably. I was a bit taken aback at this approach but, having confirmed that the caller was indeed the person he claimed to be, I wished him good night, thanked him, and proceeded next morning to follow his advice. There was, after all, nothing to lose.

We asked our solicitor to prepare an appeal, mentioned the whole business as widely as we could around the town, and—to my delight—just before our proposed deadline, we suddenly received the long-sought-after planning approval!

That was some encouragement, at least. Though, looking at the hard facts, all we had obtained was permission to build our unrealistically magnificent new nursery on land we didn't own, with money we hadn't got. But it was a little step forward and clearly we had some friends and sympathisers in high places, even if they were keeping a low profile.

By this time things were little short of desperate at

the Coach House. The dentist was becoming increasingly concerned about the state of the building, and also wanted to extend his own premises. He wanted us out soon. The mothers of handicapped children were still coming up to the, now rather weather-stained, white gate with new problems and, to cap it all, what had seemed a wonderful provision from God had turned to ashes in our mouths.

I felt I had reached the lowest ebb.

Chapter Eleven

RICHARD

Nevertheless, despite my depression, we did have a Charitable Trust and we had planning approval, for what it was worth. And people began to mention to us that perhaps we should consider raising some funds—like any other charity. Maybe we could even raise enough to build the nursery we wanted.

I didn't like the idea at all.

I had seen God provide so much in so many marvellous ways that I thought fund-raising almost indecent. Certainly some aspects I had heard about seemed almost immoral: gambling, lotteries and so on. Not the sort of thing for us at all.

But John had heard of a Christian involved in fund-raising on a national scale who had just completed a project to raise a quarter of a million pounds for the Spina Bifida Association in Liverpool.

Despite his obvious ability to tap into cash this man lived honestly and modestly, seeing his work simply in terms of helping others. I felt a little sceptical, but John was confident about his credentials, and the Spina Bifida Association knew what they were about. So I wrote off on behalf of the Trustees, asking Richard Clitheroe if he would consider discussing with us ways of helping our God-given work. I expected, even hoped, to hear nothing more.

I soon heard back. Mr Clitheroe, a retired civil servant, was fascinated by the letter, and my description of the work. He felt that if God was in this, he should come for a discussion. He did and we were all greatly impressed. He talked not of gambling or lotteries, but of existing trusts who would consider appeals, of powerful people in the country who were ready to help genuinely good causes, of bodies of concerned people who were happy to help charities in need. He knew them all and they trusted him. He would raise his own, very modest salary (agreed between us) as his first project, rather than take the usual percentage of the sum raised. And he would go on from there until an appropriate figure was in our coffers—perhaps enough to start the building-project we wanted, certainly enough to offer a decent rent for any building we might find. Convinced, we took him on; and found his enthusiasm for our work, like his humour, quite infectious.

Meanwhile, in a pub in Oldham, north-east of Manchester, at around the same time but unknown to us, a conversation was taking place that would also directly affect our fortunes.

The mother of a handicapped child who had attended at the Coach House was chatting one evening at the bar to a man who turned out to be a cameraman with Granada Television. In passing she complained that in her opinion some of the subjects of their documentaries were trivial and stupid—why didn't they take some notice of real injustice? If only they knew it, there was a story going on under their very noses—meaning the troubles we were having in

Heaton Moor. Little did she expect her comments to be taken seriously, but it wasn't long before a documentary producer was phoning Stockport Borough Council to ask about this Charnwood project. He soon found we 'didn't exist'. But producers are paid to produce, so he continued to ferret around until he found out my name.

He phoned me. Would we consider letting him do a 'quickie' five-minute documentary on our plight?

No, we wouldn't, I said. We were in enough hot water with the Local Authority as it was, without complaining about them on television.

Oh no, it would be more of an appeal for premises, he assured me. The Authority need not even be mentioned.

Reluctantly I agreed. We had never done anything like this before.

Filming day came and the Coach House, with its opportunity-group children playing happily in the garden, was the first subject of the Granada camera lens. Then the producer had an idea. Why not film the vacant plot of land for which we had just received planning approval? A picture of that would show how serious we were in our intent to continue with the work, and would round the 'piece' off nicely.

It seemed all right to me—so we all trooped off to St Paul's Road and cameras were set up near the place where John had prayed, in sight of the patch where we had projected the nursery building of our dreams. The crew were just beginning to film, intending to conclude with a shot of me explaining my hopes for this piece of land, when the side door of nearby St Paul's Church crashed open and out strode a forbidding figure.

Marching indignantly up to the producer, he demanded to know what was happening. On hearing the answer and discovering who was about to be televised, he was furious and immediately ordered us off the church land. The producer, however, held his ground and asked in reply who *he was*. To our amazement we learnt that this man was not only a member of the Parish Church Council, but also the Chairman of the Stockport Borough Council Education Committee—and he was fully aware of my 'doubtful reputation' at Charnwood!

As my tears welled up, I noticed to my horror that, unknown to us, the cameraman was filming the whole incident, and I quickly stepped out of sight.

The producer calmly continued his enquiry on the lines that if this represented the Local Authority's attitude, what were *they* doing instead for handicapped young children?

'There is nothing we can do at the moment,' was the answer. But then he noticed the camera in action and realized what was happening. Enraged, he advanced on the cameraman.

At this point the producer intervened, along with the Vicar, who had followed the Chairman out of the church unnoticed in the excitement.

They separated the warring factions and the Vicar turned to comfort me. I could see by now that this accidental meeting had blown the whole documentary sky-high, and I was therefore urgently in need of a pastoral hanky.

The Chairman turned on his heel and marched back to the comparative sanctuary of the church. Granada retreated to their broadcasting truck.

'Now, look what's happened,' I wailed. 'You've upset them all now!'

Comfortingly the producer took my arm.

'Lady, that was a gift from heaven. You'll see.'

The five-minute 'appeal' was shown straight after the election news on 8 October 1974. The camera cut from the happily playing children to the now-derelict building which we had once been offered. The commentator told the story. What would happen now to these happy children if no place could be found for them? What, in fact, was the Local Authority's view of their plight?

The stern visage of the Chairman of the Education Committee filled the screen, his status captioned neatly underneath for all to see. Nothing was included of the stormy fracas. The commentary ended with the question reiterated. What would happen?

It was a good question. John and I had a feeling that everyone on the Education Committee was watching that night and not just for the election results. The next day I waited nervously for the phone to ring, or possibly for the earth to open up and swallow me.

The call came in the evening.

'Mrs Wyatt, Director of Administration, Stockport, here. We have a property in Mauldeth Road that we understand you might be interested in leasing for the purposes of your, ah, Charity. We would be prepared to consider meeting your trustees to discuss this further, if you would wish.' I did wish and quickly phoned round with the good news. The producer had been right. It had been a gift from heaven. We were being offered the same property again.

At a later meeting the details were explained.

Basically the deal amounted to our putting everything right at our own expense, and paying rent and rates for a three-year lease. The Council would get the whole thing back at the end. Not overly

generous, you might say. But the trustees weren't
about to refuse. We had said we would take virtually
anything that was possible, we had a charity fund-
raiser at work who was familiar with this sort of
arrangement, and the location of the house couldn't
be bettered.

We accepted their terms and signed the lease. We
would move in soon after Christmas, the bulk of the
renovation work hopefully completed.

Richard Clitheroe immediately set to work, both
on fund-raising and on arranging the labour to re-
furbish the house. Convicted men sentenced to 'community service' would do the bulk of it. A number of
people would provide paint and wiring at cost price.
Then there was the clearing up of the garden—young
people from the local church would help with that
. . .

In barely six weeks Richard had the Trust on its
feet. Workers were arranged for the house and
materials ordered. To raise funds, he had visited
politicians in London, begun to make contacts with
firms, enquire about legacies and find interested
trusts. Books were started, ledgers filled in, gifts and
outgoings accounted for properly.

It was a blast of fresh air. Charnwood was on the
road to a new, brighter, future at last. Certainly the
work on the Mauldeth Road house was pretty
daunting but with dynamic Richard Clitheroe and
his experience and contacts to sort us out, we had
little to fear.

What rejoicing there was that Christmas time!
Richard, in fact, had promised to come to the
children's Christmas party at the Coach House—the
last one we would spend there—as Father Christmas.

There was great excitement among the children

that morning. Santa was coming!

But twelve o'clock came and went, and no Santa. Had Richard, the arch-organizer, forgotten this one appointment? It seemed unlikely.

The children went home disappointed. I went home to find Ann, the mothers' group host, now one of the trustees, on the doorstep.

'Grace. You'd better sit down. Betty Clitheroe phoned . . . in London . . . She's been trying to get you . . . Richard had a heart attack last night . . . on his way home. He died on the way to hospital . . .'

There was a week to Christmas.

Chapter Twelve

BIG HEARTS, SMALL MIRACLES

Of all the blows that hit us in the early days of the Charnwood Trust, I think perhaps the loss of Richard Clitheroe as a result of his heart attack was the most devastating. Certainly it was to me. So much had rested on his shoulders, so much had seemed possible because of his abilities. We had taken on the 'derelict' largely because of his expertise. True, we had had nowhere else to go and the television report had directly made it possible—but the work and the funding were all dependent upon Richard's ability alone to find us the resources—which he demonstrably could.

In the six weeks we had worked with Richard I had only begun to know the man himself and was just getting to know his family. Yet I missed him as a person—his enthusiasm, his encouragement, his presence, and his love for God. I cared deeply about Richard's wife and daughter but, to be honest, my immediate reaction was a sense of deep bitterness about our own situation.

There was the rub. If God has a plan for each of us, as we believe, this was no mere chance happening. We had to believe that God had chosen to take this man, so important to us, at that time. We had to believe that this Christmas was the right and chosen time for Richard to die. We had to accept that his death was the very best that God could do for us all.

I just could not see it. I really couldn't. I know that many people have to suffer under much greater apparent injustice—but I could not see any good reason why this had to happen.

John was kind and comforting. He was confident that things would work out for the very best. God was, and would always be, far greater than our understanding. It could not be otherwise. But I was still deeply, deeply bitter.

Why? Why? Why? It's the question we all ask at this sort of time. The mothers of handicapped children ask the same question. In a sense I knew how they felt.

Why should a loving God permit it? After endless opposition Charnwood was just about to get properly established. Richard had been God's answer to our prayers. We needed all he had to offer. Now instead of success we had a double tragedy. Instead of a nursery we had a bereaved family and a derelict building.

When I think about this sort of thing I can only conclude—and the Bible bears this out—that God does not put us here simply to do good things comfortably. The pursuit of happiness may be written into western society's constitution but in the Bible's view we are here to 'give glory to God'. That is quite a different thing. Geared to expect security and comfort, we see suffering as an unusual interruption of our ordered lives, not as the everyday occurrence which it must be in a 'fallen' world distorted by human sin and selfishness—which is what the Bible indicates our world to be. Suffering is indeed a daily experience for most of mankind—half of whom will not even have enough to eat today. 'These things are sent to try us' is a rather trite saying, but it does hold some real truth.

That was a clouded Christmas for all of us—and I would not wish that experience on anyone. But I do believe God knows what he is about (though it was very difficult to see at the time) and now, looking back, he has certainly brought about what we—and Richard—would have desired in those early days.

But why this way?

Maybe we needed to rely on God, not Richard. I don't know. But I do not think, as some have said to me, that suffering proves there can be no loving God. Suffering, pain and loss were very much part of the life of Jesus Christ; some would say the principal part. Jesus, the Son of God, 'joined in' to suffer with us and to share in all that human life entails. In his death on the cross Christ not only suffered with us, he suffered for us. And through his pain he made forgiveness and a new life possible for each of us.

Richard's death left us shocked, and full of questions and doubts. But we still trusted God although we could not see beyond the mess we were in.

What we faced was not very funny. We had no one to go to for workers or supplies—all that was to have come through Richard. Perhaps worse, we had no money to pay for them even if they came.

We had also promised the dentist we would be out of the Coach House by January. Our next term would have to start in Mauldeth Road. We could not go back on that.

We looked around to see who could help. There was one father who was a heating engineer and another who would help rig up a couple of wash-basins. All the windows needed re-glazing—perhaps John could help here—and some of the floorboards were up. We would just have to close off those rooms until the boards could be hammered home.

We made a start. The heating man came and got the heating working. Using second-hand industrial equipment, we got the basins in and one toilet working and we glazed most of the windows. A small army of fathers and husbands worked away, and it was all ready by mid-January.

So we moved in.

Floorboards were still up and there was no running hot water. Lead was missing from the roof. And we had only the limited Coach House furniture. But it was a step forward.

One morning, no more than three weeks after our move, a young smartly dressed man knocked on the door of the house and asked to be shown round. I was terrified. I thought he was an inspector from the Local Authority, and the place was, from any point of view, a shambles. But I took my courage in both hands and showed him the rooms—one for messy play (sand and water, etc.) one for quieter reading and stories, one for a small office, one nice light room upstairs for a mothers' lounge (Mauldeth Road was too far from Ann's house for her front room to be really convenient, now). This, last, was empty. He turned to me.

'Right,' he said. 'You can leave this room to me.'

Naturally I queried this rather unusual statement.

'I'm director of a furniture company,' he elaborated, not very helpfully. 'You leave it to me.'

I showed him out, not quite sure what to make of it.

What he meant, though, was soon made clear.

From then on, every so often a furniture van would draw up outside the house and the driver would unload something—a chair, a table, a couple of stools (usually they had a little chip or scratch, but otherwise they were brand new)—and then drive off. The drivers knew nothing about the pieces and there was never any delivery note. They came from all over the country.

It was a real mystery—but we were getting furnished!

A little while later the man turned up again. Then he told me the full story. He had been so entranced by the idea of the place that when he had seen what we needed he had made it a point, on his sales trips around the country, to ask suppliers if there was anything particularly shopsoiled in their warehouse—and if so would they mind popping it on the next lorry they had coming down to Stockport!

It was for a good cause, he explained.

We were so grateful. This furniture wasn't 'rubbish', by a long way—some of the best furniture gets damaged in warehouses! In fact we ended up having one room in matching named-brand dark oak and one in light! Not all at once and not all in perfect condition but pretty smart and much appreciated— by more than the mothers.

In fact small miracles like this seemed to happen most weeks. Envelopes would be shoved through the door. Someone would offer a carpet for the stairs, or some toys for the children. The money went out again almost as soon as we were given it—we were paying rent and rates and heating—but there was usually a gift just when we needed it. We lived one day at a time.

I remember one day in particular when a real

inspector was due to come and give us the once over.
The community physician, a woman doctor with
responsibility for playgroups and children's care in
the community, was coming to see us. We were very
definitely on her 'patch' and it was up to us to show
her we were doing our best.

I was concerned. It was nearly Easter, and by now
things were in better shape, but we still had nothing
to spare in the bank—which looked bad. And the
mothers' lounge, though beautifully furnished, still
had bare boards on the floor. These had been badly
vandalized and no amount of scrubbing really made
them look presentable.

I awoke that morning with a feeling of apprehen-
sion and remember praying briefly before I got up,
'Please God, if only we could have a carpet for the
mothers' room and a little bit of money, today—it
would help.' Then I got up and went down to get the
family breakfast.

About mid-morning the phone rang and the rather
worried voice of a local trainee minister came on the
line.

'Grace, I've got a problem. Sorry to trouble you,
but I don't know what to do. I'm helping to clear out
an old lady's house—she's moving to a smaller place
today—but I'm absolutely stuck to get rid of a big
carpet. I know you've got that big house in Mauldeth
Road. Could you possibly find room for it? And I'm
afraid that's not all: it's got to be right now, really—
we're in the middle of the move.'

You can imagine my feelings. When he turned up
with it and we took it upstairs it fitted perfectly—the
colour was right, the size was right. And since only
one old lady had ever walked across it, it was barely
used. The young man went away much relieved. But,

before he did so, he handed me a brown envelope, which I took to be an invitation to a church meeting. When I opened it, it contained twenty pounds. It was with confidence that I showed the doctor round that afternoon.

So it continued. One day a man in a broad flat cap walked up the drive, introduced himself, and told me he had been handicapped as a child, so he knew what it was like. He had just had an operation and could now walk properly for the first time since being a child. He was so grateful, he wanted to give us something. As we waved goodbye we opened his envelope—and counted out £500! A nurse who had stayed with us once for a meal wrote later to thank us for the hospitality. She went on: 'As I prayed about your project I felt God was telling me to give you £500 for Charnwood—but since I've never had £500 in my life I asked him to provide it for me first. Last week I received an entirely unexpected gift which has meant I can give you what I promised.'

And there in the letter was the cheque. There was also a 'PS'. 'Don't bother to thank me—*it wasn't my idea.*'

Easter came and went and I had to say that I was very grateful indeed for the way things were working out. In bits and pieces and in some surprising ways we had made good. The house was now safe and warm and the toilet and washing facilities were adequate. The rooms were carpeted (in different ways) and furnished well.

'There are just two things I would like,' I said to the helpers, half-jokingly, one Friday morning as I stood in the entrance hall waiting for the children to arrive. 'We need a tall mirror over there so that the children can see themselves as they come in the door and when they dress up. And over here I'd like a sideboard—for the lost gloves and the register and all the other bits and pieces.'

One of the helpers laughed.

'And I suppose you'll be praying for them!' she jibed.

'That'll do, that'll do!' I said, and we forgot about it in the flurry of arriving children.

Not more than half an hour later, the doorbell rang and I opened it to be confronted by a reflection of myself in a huge mirror. I was shocked and just stood there. After a few moments a man's voice piped up from behind it:

'Come on love. I can't stand 'ere all day holding this up, give us a hand.'

'Oh yes, so sorry.'

And I helped him over the threshold with the tall wardrobe-style mirror. We stood it at the end of the hall. It fitted beautifully.

'Well, er, thank you.' I ventured, still rather amazed. 'That's absolutely wonderful!'

'That ain't all, love,' he commented, as though I should know all about it. 'There's a flipping big sideboard out there too—someone's got to help!'

Actually it was rather frightening, if the truth be told. I won't tell you what our helper said when she came back into the hallway. At first she thought it was a put-up job. But it wasn't. I really had no idea that anything was due that morning.

God's help for us did not stop at bringing along bits and pieces. He got to work on people too.

One of the other problems we had faced on moving was that faithful Irene—who had been with us from the Dean Road days—had had to leave. Her husband had moved his work and this took them out of the area. This had left a major gap in the day-to-day running of the nursery. The mums and helpers were good, and Erica Vere still provided tremendous support, as did Kay, Joan and Brenda—three other part-timers who had all been parents of Charnwood children. But I really needed a trained and experienced teacher for overall control and direction—a deputy for me. I was, after all, responsible for 100 children by now. Added to which getting the whole place ship-shape had taken up all my energies and it was often as much as I could do to concentrate on the children as well. So I looked around urgently for someone to take Irene's place.

I was in the supermarket when I met Mary, whose young child had been at Charnwood. I knew her as the rapidly promoted head of a local infant school—a high flyer in children's education by all accounts and something of a star in the Local Authority's eyes. She drew me aside and questioned me searchingly about Irene's role and responsibilities at Charnwood. I told her all about it—she was a fellow educationalist and it was a good opportunity for me to explain what we were doing to someone so obviously destined for high responsibility.

But when I had finished she looked at me rather shyly: 'Grace, if I applied for Irene's job would you consider me for it?'

I was appalled.

'Mary, you can't be serious! There's no money in it for a start. You're used to a professional salary. We could offer virtually nothing compared with that—and then only if we get it as a gift! You've a very bright future ahead of you. What about your career?'

'Oh, no I mean it. I want to give up my job. I think

what Charnwood is doing is very important. In any case I need a lighter job as my mother's health is deteriorating and she needs care. Would you consider me?'

The trustees met and considered her offer. They concluded that if she was quite sincerely prepared to make the sacrifice, knowing what she was getting into, then we would be silly not to accept her offer.

She felt very strongly it was what she wanted to do and her family supported her in this. The Local Authority was frankly aghast at her proposed resignation—and her intentions. They put many obstacles in her way, thinking her decision disastrous. Materially it certainly seemed so; and as to a lighter job, that too would prove to be an illusion. But Mary remained adamant. They agreed to accept her resignation.

So in early summer she became my deputy, and what an amazing help she was. Initially she declined to get involved with the handicapped children but before long she was avidly studying their needs, and reading widely. As the connection with the university had slowly given us medical credibility (and continues to do so), so Mary's presence gave us academic and educational acceptance—and, through that, came a slow thawing in the frozen attitude of the Local Authority for whom Mary had once worked. She was, in my book, a wonderful gift from God in every sense and became deeply immersed in the purpose and direction of the work. We had needed her badly—as we had needed so much.

That summer I was grateful—still mystified, but grateful—and no longer bitter. Despite the tragedy, which hung over us still, all was very far from being lost.

Chapter Thirteen

LEARNING TOGETHER

As the word spread that we were still 'in business', other mothers found their way to our door. New children continually kept arriving, though no one was being recommended by doctors. Our understanding of children, their conditions and problems was now more sophisticated than it had been with Nina and Nicholas. We had been pretty green when they had been put in our charge. Now we had not only experience but a considerable amount of study behind us. Although our basic approach was the one we had originally developed—integrating handicapped and normal children together in a caring environment—our care for the mother as well as child, and the techniques of instructive play and educational development for those specifically handicapped, were now more advanced. The story of just one of the handicapped children we came across at Mauldeth Road shows the increase in confidence and skill we had gained by this time.

Jane was a tiny little girl with Down's Syndrome. Her mother already had wide experience of medical social work and knew all about the usual provision of such children by the authorities. Neither parent wanted Jane to go to a nursery just for handicapped children. They asked the Health Visitor if she knew of any place where normal and handicapped children could learn and play.

So the Health Visitor rang me one day to explain. 'Would you please see them?' she asked.

I was intrigued by the mother's independent attitude and arranged for her to bring Jane to visit us. As usual that afternoon the playroom was full of busy, noisy children. Upstairs in the lounge a group of mothers had withdrawn from the activity to relax over a cup of tea.

Jane was a round-faced little girl with an alert expression enhanced by two baby plaits. Together we looked into all the rooms and I briefly described what was going on. Perhaps they would care to come again another day, I suggested as they were leaving.

So I was delighted when Jane's mother phoned me at home that evening wanting to arrange a further visit. Then she became distressed. Had she left it too late?

No, I reassured her, the time was just right.

As we got to know Jane we soon found she was short-sighted and needed glasses. In her determination to fix pegs into peg-board holes she almost had her nose against the board!

We also noticed that her mouth muscles were rather slack.

'Does she chew properly?' we asked.

'She doesn't chew at all,' her mother told us. 'She's afraid because she tends to choke, and she won't eat any solid food at all.'

Something had to be done about this. So, with her mother's approval (as long as she didn't have to watch the performance), Mary and I set to work! Jane's favourite food was fruit yoghurt. This, we decided, would be her reward for chewing—but chewing what?

'TUC' crackers were our inspiration. Crunchy to bite on, they would quickly crumble and dissolve in the mouth if chewing proved impossible! We decided on a ten-day programme.

Jane was duly settled into a small chair behind a low table facing us and the door was firmly closed against intruders. One piece of cracker was pushed between her lips and, when that had been swallowed, a spoonful of yoghurt was offered as a reward. Splutters, chokes and muffled screams followed— and persisted during each brief session for nine consecutive days.

Worn down by the strain and anxiety, we decided that 'day ten' must be the last. Resolutely we entered the dreaded room together, to Jane's squeaks of despair, or perhaps annoyance. We sat her as usual at the table. After a moment's uncertainty, she turned towards the TUC cracker in Mary's hand and opened her mouth. Amazingly she bit off a small portion and duly crunched it, turning to the yoghurt for her reward. Cracker and yoghurt were quickly demolished.

Jane rapidly became one of Charnwood's best 'chewers', even tackling a large cold-beef sandwich on a train outing with us to London some time later.

Children with Down's Syndrome are called slow learners but it's by no means true of all of them, nor for all areas of learning. Jane soon became a competent reader and an even more articulate speaker. From her early days with us, we discovered she had a logical mind and when, at the age of four, she was asked to repeat something for a psychologist who wanted to demonstrate her verbal understanding, she firmly told him it wouldn't be necessary: 'I've done it once and I won't do it again!'

Unbelievably, she regularly read *The Times* and became well-informed on current affairs. She closely followed the case of Dr Arthur who was prosecuted for failing to save the life of a 'Down's' baby.

'Was that baby like me?' she asked her mother.

She progressed through primary to secondary education. Now, in a local comprehensive school, she can tell her class all about her condition. Among other subjects, she is learning two European languages!

The birth of most babies with Down's Syndrome causes their parents a period of great anguish and distress; so much prejudice surrounds their early life. But each one is an individual with potential for a happy relationship with his or her family and friends. Some, like Jane, also have vital personalities and a range of academic skills. It was Dr Albert Segal who first insisted publicly that 'no child is ineducable'. We completely agree, but our experience has also convinced us that the content of that education must be enhanced by the setting in which it is carried out.

The stimulation, example and challenge that normal children offer to parents and to handicapped children must never be denied them in the name of 'special education'. Individual tuition will be necessary if these children are to learn individual skills. But the ordinary experiences of play with normal children provide the essential motivation to master and to use these skills in the right place. Even the most severely handicapped young children seem brighter and happier through responding to the smile and chatter of normal play-partners. And the normal children are stimulated as well!

One of the children, Owen, had been watching Robert, a boy with cerebral palsy, having his legs exercised, and had noticed how we then encouraged him to crawl. One evening at home, when he was sitting in the bath, inspiration dawned on Owen. He shouted for his mum to bring him paper and pencil. The bemused mum then watched him draw a diagram of what Robert needed.

Next day at Charnwood he told us what to do. 'You take some sticks and hammer them into a frame like this,' he said, 'and then you tie on the batteries behind Robert's knees. Then when they're switched on he'll be able to walk.'

Owen's mother, happy to be involved, told us full details of this invention. We have always found it important to bring the mothers in on the serious problem of integration.

The present Charnwood Trustees have recently appointed a physiotherapist. Her job will be teaching mothers how to manage their children, and teaching our staff to do the same. No physiotherapist can possibly treat a handicapped child adequately in two twenty-minute sessions a week—the average arrangement in hospital. What is needed is therapy every day—maybe several times a day. It must be part of the total management of the child—sitting, feeding, playing. The mothers may not be trained 'physios' but each can learn the essentials of helping her own child—and then she can spend the time needed in the best possible environment, that of her own home!

Not all medical advisers would agree with these ideas. Some paediatricians are apparently depressed at having to tell parents that their child is less than perfect. They often pass on their gloom to the parents, even hinting that perhaps it would have been better had the unborn child been aborted—or later allowed to die. Some still say about a child, 'nothing can be done . . .' and leave the parents with that disastrous conclusion.

Happily most parents determine to try at least to do 'something'. Barbara—now one of our staff—and her husband Alan adopted Jacob as their sixth child. Medical opinion was critical of them, as Jacob has severe spina bifida and would therefore never walk or do anything worthwhile.

Fortunately his five brothers and sisters did not hear the medical views, and treated their Jake just as they would any other younger brother!

His parents worked intensively with him in the evenings, exercising his legs and giving him lots of experiences suggested by the physiotherapist.

In Charnwood nursery, we noticed Jake's legs growing longer and stronger until one day, when he thought we weren't watching, he stood. Eventually Jake walked into the paediatrician's consulting-room, to the doctor's shock and delight. Immediately X-rays were taken and it was found that, amazingly, Jake had grown two normal hip joints, and there were signs of increasing sensation in his legs. Jake has now been successfully integrated into his normal primary school near home.

From a simple concept of care, we now find ourselves offering a complex and sophisticated 'therapy'. And we are still learning.

We also never overlook the fact that for each handicapped child coming to Charnwood, there are two or three others who come solely for their early learning and play experiences.

We are not running a playgroup only for handicapped children.

Charnwood is for *all* children.

Chapter Fourteen

FAMILY MATTERS

From the time we started the very first playgroup, John and I had felt we were involved, not only in 'helping out the mums', or 'getting the children together', or even 'integrating handicapped children' but also in a small way in God's work—and principally God's work for the family.

As a playgroup it was through the children that we made contact with the mums and dads. But some of these contacts brought to light such family predicaments that we were often turned to for advice and guidance by the parents. Whatever the problem—and there were some very deep and bitter ones—the essence was usually a conflict of relationships, a lack of stability or feeling of worth, within a marriage or family. Such problems were obviously more liable to arise in families with a handicapped child, although in some cases it had the opposite effect. The contrast with the two dozen or so happy Christian families we mixed with each weekend made us want to share the recipe.

Yet despite our own beliefs, at Charnwood (even today) we do not make any attempt, unsolicited, to thrust our Christian views on those with whom we come in contact, be it parents in need, children, government officials, doctors, health officials, students, volunteers, or whoever. Many, perhaps most, of those whose children, normal or handicapped, come to Charnwood know little if anything about our history, or our basis as a Christian charity. If someone wants to look deeper, to ask about our approach, our views, we tell them. If not, we keep quiet.

Nevertheless, down the years, there has been a steady trickle of parents who have turned up at Charnwood carrying a child, who have eventually—often after many months or years—come to the point of personal encounter with God. Experiences like these are life-changing.

Christians often speak of Jesus Christ as their 'saviour': someone who has saved them from the guilt and penalty of their sins. But we are 'saved' from many other things too: and we know those who have been saved from miserable, mixed up—even addicted—lives by the power of Christ. Like so much at Charnwood, many of these stories, if we did not know them to be true, would sound unbelievable. Some, even now years later, are too emotive and too sensitive to speak about. But one family's story we can share.

We came across the Bridges just about the time we were settling into our fourth temporary 'home' at Mauldeth Road.

I was put in touch with a family whose little three-year-old girl, Joanne, had been diagnosed as having a malignant tumour on the brain. She had already spent nine months of her short life in hospital, undergoing brain surgery for the removal of most of this growth and then having radio-therapy, it was hoped, to destroy what remained.

She was brought out of hospital very weak, with much of her hair shaved off, and apparently almost sightless. She was often distraught and found it difficult to sleep, probably because of having had constant treatment at regular intervals night and day.

Over the telephone, the Health Visitor was pretty blunt, saying that Joanne was quite likely to die; in fact it was incredible that she had not died before this.

Her parents, a professional couple who now took care of her at home, found themselves under great strain. The child cried or whined frequently, day and night, and had little appetite.

'Could you do something—anything at all?' I was asked. 'Maybe the atmosphere at your playgroup might help?'

'Of course. We'll see her, with her mother—right away,' I said.

The social worker who contacted me had not been exaggerating. What a pathetic creature Joanne was! Little stick-like legs, scant hair, sightless eyes and (we had been warned), an almost permanent wail!

To begin with Joanne's grizzling cast something of a blight over the whole place. But little by little, day by day, as she sat on her mother's knee in the middle of it all, we noticed her interest move from one noise to another—as Nina's had done at the Coach House. And then her eyes followed! Was there some sight there, after all?

At last, one day as she sat on the floor, something was so very interesting that she made a move towards it on her own—and a little later actually dragged herself up on her two unsteady legs and began to walk.

And the crying had stopped.

From then on, improvements continued and in a short time we realized that her hospital therapy had been effective. She was on the way to recovery.

During her long months of painful treatment in hospital, her loss of sight, and the despair she no doubt heard in the voices of the nurses and her parents, Joanne had become very depressed and almost lost the will to live.

As she got much better, her mother caught up with me one morning and asked to have a chat.

'I've never told you about Joanne, have I?' she asked. No, she hadn't, I confirmed. Did she want to now? I asked her into my room for coffee, and there Kathy told me her story.

When Joanne was in hospital undergoing all her treatment, she had seemed so close to death that on several occasions, when the doctors had said she wouldn't last the night, Kathy had called a priest to give the child a final blessing. She had been brought up a Roman Catholic, she explained, and she felt this was the right and proper thing to do—despite her husband's doubts about God.

What had intrigued her at the time was another young mother, just across the ward, in a similar situation to herself, with a dying child. She always seemed so calm and could even smile. She obviously had some special sort of inner peace. The day after Joanne's final crisis, Kathy determined to find out more about this other mum. So she marched across and demanded to know what she was reading. Was it something religious, or what? And how could she be so calm?

It turned out that she was reading the Bible. Kathy decided on the spot that she must look more closely into this. She went straight out of the hospital and found a shop. There she bought, not one Bible but two (there were several modern translations available), just to make sure she got 'the right one'.

'So,' she said. 'I began to read it—and—it began to help! What is more, I began to pray about Joanne . . !'

Suddenly she stopped in mid-flow and looked at me intently.

'Sorry,' she said. 'Perhaps it all seems silly to you. Can you understand?'

I smiled. 'I can indeed. It makes a great deal of sense to me.' I went on to explain a little of my own beliefs and trust in God.

'Oh,' she enthused. 'How wonderful! I should like to talk to you more about this—but John, my husband, perhaps wouldn't understand.'

'Well,' I said, 'don't worry—we'll all be praying for you anyway. Come and talk again when you feel you can.'

The interesting, and unexpected, interview was at an end.

But matters did not end there. Not at all. For very soon Kathy's husband started to bring Joanne along to the group himself.

This was largely the result of her amazing progress. By now she could definitely see, her hair had grown again, she was walking all the time and was eating well. So we felt she was ready to come to the morning group and this allowed Dad to do the honours.

Quite often he stayed for a chat. We discussed all manner of controversial issues. And my Christian perspective on things led to some amazement.

'How can you, an educated, responsible person,

etc, etc, take the concept of God seriously?'

We had several discussions about the evidence for God—for the life of Jesus—for the resurrection of Jesus. Then John and I were invited by the Bridges to an evening meal. We went, and we laugh about it now, because we nearly didn't have a meal at all! Neither of them had time to go to the kitchen to finish cooking and serving it. The discussion started almost on the doormat—and it lasted until the early hours, with an invitation to a further session soon.

It became apparent that it was John, the so-called agnostic, who was most seriously hungry for truth. Starting as he did from an apparently 'scientific' conviction that 'there's probably nothing there,' he nevertheless seemed honestly willing to accept viewpoints different from his own—provided they were convincing. For us, therefore, it was a logical matter. We had simply (and at some length) to set before him the truth, the evidence as we and other Christians had seen and experienced it, and let him draw his own conclusions.

Kathy however was in a different position—trying to connect her own searching of the Bible and her personal experiences with half-forgotten Roman Catholic traditions—and becoming more confused than satisfied with the results.

Eventually one evening John came round to return to us what he said was the fortieth book he had read that discussed some aspect of Christ or a personal Christian faith. Missionary stories, histories, Bible commentaries, biographies—he had devoured them all; many suggested by us, others sought out from the local library.

He came in, sat down and said: 'I have to say that I am now quite satisfied in my own mind, intellectually, that all you have said—all *these* have said (and here he swept his arm towards our bookshelves in the lounge)—holds true.

'But,' he continued, 'becoming a Christian is a matter for the will, too, isn't it? A matter of commitment, of stepping out, of surrender, of putting myself in God's hands . . . all that. I'm scared of that.

'It is true, yes,' he sighed. 'But it is not true *for me* . . . yet.'

It was obvious to us, then, that there was no need for more argument.

We promised to pray. And we also put them in touch with a close friend who went along to an active, Christ-centred church near where they lived (a family who themselves had a handicapped child at Charnwood). They quickly formed a friendship, with so much in common.

One morning, early, I had a phone call. It was from John Bridge.

'Grace!' he shouted down the phone, his voice distorted by the volume. 'Grace! It happened last night!'

Now at 8 a.m. I am not at my best—though, to be honest, I had a pretty good idea what he meant.

'What John?'

'I did it, Grace! I gave my life to Christ! But,' he added quietly, 'I'm still scared stiff.'

I thanked God with him over the phone and re-assured him. I would have been more worried, I said, had he *not* felt a little awed and shaken by a meeting with God!

Kathy too had come to a point of decision, re-solving her own confusions—seeing clearly at last the vital difference between the outward trappings of faith and the wonder of the real thing.

Since then they have played a growing role in their local church and in the work of Charnwood. John, in fact, is now one of the Charnwood trustees. Joanne is a lovely teenager. And Kathy, with two more children to care for, now shows as a mother the peace of Christ which she so much envied in another, in those dark days at the hospital.

The Bridges' story is just one of many. Not all have a happy ending like theirs. I am sure they would be the first to say that Christ never promised his followers that their lives would be a bed of roses. They have had their fair share of troubles down the years. The difference, of course, is that they know Jesus is in there with them. The picture of the life of faith as a 'walk with God' is a good one. There is someone by your side; an extra member of the family. And God's offer is open to everyone who turns to him. There is nothing exclusive about it. It is not for special people only. Each of us has the choice. To listen or not. It is always my prayer that those whom we meet and talk to at Charnwood, and at our home, will see something of God's work in our lives—and will want to know more for themselves.

Chapter Fifteen

ROLL OUT THE BARREL

Meantime, with the workload increasing almost daily, I was beginning to be in need of another teacher—and a secretary. Someone mentioned to me that the then newly-formed Manpower Services Commission had new arrangements for paying professional people professional rates, if there was work to do but (as in our case) there were insufficient funds.

I got in touch with them and arranged to set up a scheme to employ the two people I needed. As for the teacher, I knew the one I wanted. Helen was already working with us, voluntarily. A quick, confirming interview and the arrangements were complete.

But a secretary. That was a bit different. I'd never had one before and had a list of requirements for such a person that was pretty demanding. She had to be capable of being a Personal Assistant when I was away from the office working with the children, to be able to play the piano in case of musical 'emergencies' (we couldn't operate without music from the piano!), and she had to be in sympathy with the aims of Charnwood—which included Christian sympathies, if possible.

The MSC sent me dozens of applicants; the

number was a sad reflection on the employment situation. But I knew what I wanted, and eventually chose an efficient girl, Diane, who loved the work and got on with the job. I was very pleased, even if her piano-playing was minimal!

However, my critical selection procedure had, apparently, given me something of a reputation in the MSC office. Perhaps we were a stranger bunch than we had first seemed, thought the worthy officials. Perhaps we were using the MSC scheme for undisclosed and unworthy ends. Maybe the conditions of work were poor and degrading—after all, the MSC had had enough lambasting in the press about encouraging 'slave' labour and so on. They had better take a look.

So, in due course, I found myself opening the door of the nursery to a formally-dressed gentleman from the MSC, who courteously informed me that he was 'just taking a look round, seeing how things were'.

I showed him everything, and he seemed content. I then asked him upstairs for a coffee and chat, to conclude the visit. He sat down in the tiny office (on a chair that had appeared out of a van from Stoke on Trent), and I sat down at my desk (recently offloaded from Manchester University). Diane brought us both some coffee and was briefly subjected to an interrogation on her present employment, job satisfaction, etc.

The official stretched his legs and commented on the lovely scrolled Bible text fixed on the wall above my desk. It was a present from a couple with a handicapped child in Aberystwyth who had once visited us: 'If you abide in me, and my words abide in you, then I will give you what you ask'—words of Jesus, from the Gospel of John.

Underneath it I had pinned one page of the 'dream' plans we had so foolishly asked to be drawn up earlier. It seemed to me an appropriate juxtaposition. Hopes and dreams—very much God's province.

'Thinking of building a place, then, are you?' He nodded at the blueprint.

I waved a dismissive hand. 'Oh, we hope to, one day. But we've got no money.' My heart dipped as I spoke. The memory of Richard was still painful.

'Looked at any land, then?'

'No . . . o, not really. Well, yes, actually. We've seen one plot but it's too expensive. Humph! even cheap it would be too expensive,' I commented wrily.

'Planning? Have you got planning permission?' he pressed.

I told him we had.

'D'you want us to build it for you, then?' he shot back without blinking.

'We could run to labour costs of about . . .' he paused and eyed the plan speculatively, 'about £100,000. What do you say?'

I had switched off by this time, totally confused. I stared blankly at him for a moment, then at the wall. The text ran, unregistered, through my head a couple of times.

'I think,' I said slowly, 'that you had better talk to my husband. He's a civil engineer. I'm sure he would understand what you are talking about. I'm afraid I don't.'

He left, courteously and officially—and got in touch with John. John explained later what was happening. The man had a number of responsibilities aside from checking up on doubtful schemes and employers. One of them was to find projects in the north-west which merited the (MSC supported) attentions of unemployed bricklayers, plumbers, decorators and so on. He felt that the building of our 'day centre' would be too good an opportunity to miss. It had all the right qualifications: size, relevance and 'community interest'—something, apparently, of prime importance to the MSC. If we could buy the land and materials they would pay men to do the job. It was virtually all agreed.

The trustees looked at this and prayed—then went ahead and signed the papers! All Charnwood had to do was to provide the picks and the shovels and the bricks and the fencing and the land and . . . everything (the cost of which was conservatively estimated to equal that of the labour). Work was due to start one month after the ink had dried on the paper. It was incredible.

The immediate consequences were, of course, that we had a major building project dumped in our lap. And it was soon made clear to us that the men we were about to employ on it were—quite naturally— the least employable of the bricklaying, plumbing and electrical work force of the north-west. John told me that our first and most urgent need (apart from funds) was a strong, experienced, but understanding site manager.

So we sent the word out for an unemployed site manager—and several applied for the job. A small committee, including myself, met each man and interviewed him, reviewing his credentials. The first shock was their previous salaries. They were astronomical! We immediately doubled what the MSC had intended to offer, but even that didn't come near to what was apparently expected.

The interviewees came and went, none seeming

quite the man we were looking and praying for.

One of the last of the day was Brian Smith. Brian wore the sort of clothes that made you reach for your sunglasses before taking a second look. His check suit and vivid tie did not, we felt, mark him out as one appropriate to handle building for the sober and serious-minded Charnwood project. (After all, we had just 'soberly' signed up to build a day centre without land or materials!)

But as we spoke we uncovered an interesting story. Brian had had two wonderful marriages, he told us. His first wife had, sadly, died of cancer and his second wife, whom he had recently married, was every bit as marvellous as the first. He felt so grateful that he wanted to 'give something back' for all this happiness. He would accept a lower salary and he really wanted to build the best day centre for children in the whole of Stockport—if not of Britain!

His steel-tipped shoes glittered in the afternoon sun. We looked at his references. They were good. He had built hospitals and day centres—all sorts—in the past. His orange socks stood out against the pastel shade of the blue carpet. He certainly would be a 'different' appointment.

We all agreed: he was the one.

'He looks like a "spiv" and nothing more,' said a helper who had seen him come in for interview, when I told her. 'You must be mad. You'll regret it. You will.'

We would see. But we had first to buy the land and the equipment before Brian had a building site to manage. Still, the contract was signed. We could now say we were going ahead with the building. People might support that. It was something tangible. But these things take time to organize. Even assuming the (rapidly learning) band of trustees could get a campaign together, it would still take time. From an objective point of view, what was needed was a single gift to 'launch' us on our way.

We looked first at acquiring the land. We knew it was for sale and the asking price ran to five figures. But it was totally boxed off by other people's gardens and the only access was that offered exclusively to us. We decided to bargain. The price came down, slowly. We explained what we intended to use the land for, the situation with the access, that we were a charity, and so on. The price dropped to what it was really worth—about a third of what had been originally asked.

At that price one of the trustees said she could personally make available an interest-free loan for the whole sum. Nothing like supporting your own charity! She did, and we purchased the land. Over the first hurdle!

All fairly straightforward—except for the fact that some local shopkeepers decided to get up a petition against us and our project. They did not want little handicapped children around in the streets. It might affect the neighbourhood.

'It's a great work—but not here.' How often has that been said? Happily the petition failed because of greater local support for our work.

We pressed on. Now for bricks and mortar.

One day, two senior men from Lanchester Taverns (Wilson Breweries) called to see me. It seemed they had decided that, since it was the year of the Queen's Jubilee, they were going to have a special charity appeal. They were looking for a local charity with a major project they could support. They felt they would be able to raise around £3,000,

so the project must be something big. They had
contacted us because our name had been added (by a
secretary who personally knew of our work) to the
bottom of a list of known charities presented to the
Board of Directors for their consideration. They
were intrigued. What was Charnwood? And why had
this name been added to the list at the last minute?

I sat the two men down (under the now very
relevant drawings and very relevant Bible text) and
offered them coffee.

They outlined their plans. But I must confess I was
rather cool about the idea. The offer was great, their
concern was great. But a brewery as backer? Hmm,
this was a poser. A good many of our strongest
Christian supporters—who had been with us from
the start, praying for us and giving to us when we had
needed it so badly—would have reservations about
such a sponsor. They were staunch friends and,
frankly, we owed them a sincere debt of gratitude. I
frowned.

'You're not happy, Mrs Wyatt. What's the
matter?' queried the executive. Then he put two and
two together. 'Ah, you think we will be making
alcoholics in support of your cause?'

I mumbled something about it not quite being
that, but . . .

'Well, you don't need to worry. We're sponsoring
a parachute jump, by all our publicans. It will be the
biggest thing in the north-west, you'll see.'

I thanked them but explained that I would have to
see the trustees. I knew this decision would be something of a watershed for us. We would, in the future
(assuming the new centre was built), be receiving
money from all sorts of people and organizations,
some in our eyes obviously genuine and worthy,

some less clearly so. What would we do? So the trustees met, and they came up with a formula that we have stuck to ever since. Provided the money was not stolen, or the product of criminal or 'shady' dealing, as far as we knew, we would accept it—as long as there were no strings attached. But we would never *apply* for donations of money associated with gambling or anything similar.

It was perhaps a fine line to draw—and though it may sound a rather elastic decision, it is a principle which has led us to refuse substantial sums on occasion. We refused to apply for a town lottery donation some time later—although we urgently needed a roof—and we were told the money was there for the asking.

So, with the policy now clear, I said 'yes' to the brewery and, confident of the success of their Jubilee appeal, we went ahead and bought the first load of equipment. Brian, now in a portacabin on site, hired his first gang of men.

John arranged to try out a civil engineering computer programme on the work, to organize the ordering of men and materials as the project progressed and control the costs. We wanted no idle hands or wasted money. Work was started—and Lanchester landlords and bar ladies went into parachute training, possibly regretting the ardour with which their patron company supported the monarchy and their local charities. The day came for the presentation of the cheque. It was a grand affair shown on television and for us none too soon, for bills were already waiting to be paid.

Two of the brewery directors pedalled all the way from their head office to the centre on a tandem, to present us with their collected 'earnings'. The television crews followed them along and zoomed in with glee as I smilingly accepted the cheque for a staggering £5,100 *engraved on the specially painted lid of a beer barrel*!

Our faithful teetotal friends looked askance for a moment—but we were happy and content. We had been offered the money. God had provided, we knew.

The barrel lid is still in Charnwood. It hangs on the wall inside the entrance, a proud memento of the first step forward in building the new centre.

That hot summer's night, as I lay in bed recalling the events of the day and offering up quiet thanks, I thought, just for a moment, I heard a low rumbling chuckle from heaven. But I expect it was only distant thunder.

Chapter Sixteen

SITE FOR SORE EYES

We were glad we had chosen Brian Smith, *very* glad. He saw us through thick and thin, summer and winter (twice), poverty and plenty.

The men on the site proved to be all that John had predicted, and worse. Some of them seemed to have come straight out of Strangeways prison. Some came to us only to return there. Tools were stolen, equipment was stolen, workmen were sometimes surly and violent. But Brian remained on top. Not always without a scratch, though.

He came in one morning to find that the pipework, so carefully laid the day before for all our complex plumbing, had been ripped up in the night. Unlike us, he did not immediately suspect vandals. He nosed around the site and discovered, unofficially, and without evidence, that the very workmen who had laid the pipes had removed them again overnight! For sale or what, he did not know, but regretfully he decided we needed a guard dog—against our own men!

One was found and his handler assured us that he was more than adequate for the task of guardian. So it proved when Brian arrived on site to start the next morning's work and the dog, unable to tell friend from foe, leapt out at him, ignoring his master's commands, and sank his teeth into Brian's arm, biting right through his tough leather jacket and pinning him to the floor of his cabin.

The handler was horrified and pulled the dog away bodily. He was hopelessly apologetic.

'Please, sorr, I'm sorry. I really am. I'll get another dog. 'Twill be no trouble. Please Mr Smith, sorr, I need the work.'

Brian, his arm throbbing with pain, amazingly relented and accepted the offer. I was in the porta-cabin checking over some details when the man returned with a large Alsatian.

'This 'ere's Storm, Mr Smith, sorr,' he introduced. ''E'll not bite ya'. You'll 'ave no trouble wi' Storm, I promise.' With that he opened the dog's mouth. He hadn't a tooth in his head!

Having been assured that his bark, however, was substantially worse than his bite we took on Storm and his master as joint night guardians of the property.

We discovered a little later that Storm's master—along with a good number of the work-force—was rather overfond of his drink. Unlike the others, however, he was being paid to sit around for most of the time, making the occasional foray on patrol before returning to the snug protection of his night-watchman's hut. Thus he tended to doze off, after an early-evening session with his cans and bottles, rather than remain alert and perform hourly rounds of the site, as agreed with Brian.

The watchman's solution to his own drowsiness was to put Storm on a very long lead and let him roam the site at will. This permitted his handler, with a reasonably good conscience, to settle down for fifty or more winks in the hut.

One day Brian informed me that the watchman had had to take some time out to go to hospital. He had hurt his face. Had he been attacked by intruders, I queried, worried for the poor man.

Well, yes and no. Brian explained.

Early in the small hours, as far as he could tell, someone had tried to break into the site (which was surrounded by a stout fence). Faithful old Storm, on his wandering lead, had heard them and, barking madly, had frightened them off. But Storm was not a dog to reflect too much on the fact that out of sight was actually out of site—and that he could therefore relax, secure in the knowledge that he had fully answered the call of duty. Instead he determined on pursuit to finish the job, or perhaps in order to sink his gums into something more rewarding than his (texturized) soyabean dog food.

He was, however, still attached to his sleeping master. This unfortunate individual was rudely awakened, not by barking but by a powerful jerk on his wrist—to which he had firmly secured the dog's lead.

Half dazed, he was then hauled bodily from his chair, out of the door and, face down, across the rough earth and gravel of the building site. He barely managed to arrest his progress (and that of his distant companion) by determinedly wedging his foot in a passing pile of breeze blocks.

The dawn revealed a very sober and much-scarred watchman, armed with an epic story of midnight mayhem in which he, and to a certain extent Storm, had successfully fought off a massed attack by a band of merciless cut-throat hooligans who had invaded the site. And could he go home now, via the hospital?

And shouldn't he be paid more for the danger he was running?

The real story was discovered pretty quickly by a barely straight-faced Brian. Storm and his master returned, after treatment, to their duties. It was noted thereafter that Storm had a shorter lead.

Although some incidents were comical, some were not; and we were always aware of the tremendous pressure of responsibility as each stage of the building was completed. We were responsible to the Trust for the success of the projects; we were also responsible to all those who had given us time and money—all the children, present and future, whom we hoped would benefit so much from this, literally 'purpose-built' facility; and we were responsible to the MSC and the labourers. It was a heavy load and entailed daily visits to the site by John to check and advise. Derek, the site clerk, also put in stalwart work, complaining almost daily about Storm's dog-hairs in his files, but providing regular computerized costings which bowled over the MSC inspectors who'd seen nothing like them.

Also, unseen by others, were our daily appeals to God for strength and wisdom. It became a precious weekly routine for John and me, early on Saturday mornings, to make our way to the deserted site, go in through the rough, vacant doorway, up the un-finished stairs and into the small bare room at the back. There, alone together, amid the dusty debris and cast-down tools, looking out over the heaped-up earth and disordered equipment of the site, we would thank God for his goodness to date and ask for his help with, and provision for, the next phase, the next item, the next need in his project.

God's help and people's giving did not always

come in terms of cash. Quite a lot came in 'kind'.

I remember, towards the later stages of the building—which was overrunning the schedule badly because the labourers had realized, rightly, that the longer they took to build the place the longer they would be in employment—going to speak to a local women's group.

John and the rest of the family were annoyed that I had to go out again in the evening. I was doing too much, they said. I was running the group at Mauldeth Road, popping over to the building site, raising money by appeals and concerts (Cliff Richard gave two for our benefit, and became our Patron), and so on. Couldn't I stay in for one evening and rest?

Well, yes, I could—but not tonight. I had promised to go and speak, so I would.

'All right, but you really mustn't stay too late,' cautioned John. 'Anyway where are you going?'

'The Bored and the Broke!' I threw back at him as I closed the door. It was true—that's what this women's group called themselves. In reality, although they must have been a bit bored to invite me along as a diversion, they certainly weren't broke—not judging by the casual way gold and silver jewellery worn by the audience flashed in front of me, and leaving aside the size of the private house in which I was speaking.

I gave them my best, which perhaps wasn't too good, as it seemed to me the evening was wasted in an unnecessary discussion about staff shortage and the wages those who worked at Charnwood were getting. I explained as well as I could. Committed people are sometimes prepared to make real sacrifices of money, and other things, when they think it important. But everyone seemed intent on missing the point.

Perhaps, I thought vaguely, these women might be broke in some ways.

At about eleven o'clock I called things to a halt and thanked them all for their attention. I was tired and rather depressed as I walked out of the large, ornate room. John had been right. I should not have come. Then, just as I got to the back of the room, I noticed a small woman motioning at me. I stopped. She spoke quietly over the hum of conversation.

'Do you need any tiles?' she asked.

I looked blank—which was getting to be a habit.

'My husband said to ask—do you need any tiles for the building?' she repeated, amplifying her question.

I still couldn't think, but I pulled out a piece of paper and wrote down her name and telephone number, promising to pass on her husband's offer to the right quarters. I thanked her, and escaped into the night.

Next day I passed the note on to our architect and thought no more about it.

Several weeks later a lorry turned onto the site and began to unload. There was box after box of tiles. I looked at the delivery note: the cost of each batch was itemized down the side. The total came to four figures. But across the whole bill was written in big letters, NO CHARGE.

It seemed that our architect had placed an order.

Now of course, when you work with children, tiles are useful things to have around and he had seen this a good while back. Tiles for the kitchen area, tiles for the washrooms and bath area, tiles for the sandpit, and so on. So he had contacted the woman's husband and had outlined his requirements, and here it all was. Old stock, apparently, from Pilkington's vast glassworks—but bright and new, and ideal for us. What a gift!

There was a particularly interesting rider to this, and it shows just how carefully, how precisely, God cared for us during that time.

Not long after, we were hunting round for a sink unit for the kitchen area. I thought that we might find (as so often seemed to happen) a local store with a shopsoiled unit they would let us have at a reduced cost. I asked around and was delighted to be invited to come and have a look in the basement of a builders' merchant shop that had an 'old sink unit knocking around somewhere down there'. I went over to see it. Sure enough, there was an old, but unused, sink and drainer.

It looked fine. How much did he want for it? The owner hummed and hawed and then fell to musing as he looked about at the other things that stood around in his basement. On impulse he pointed to a fitted kitchen range, with cupboards and hob and oven—a complete kitchen in fact—sitting, rather dustily, in the corner.

'That's been here a long time too,' he said, 'you can have that if you like—if it will fit.'

Again I asked how much. He told me. He would give us the whole lot for barely the price of a new cooker.

We rushed back and measured up. It fitted, perfectly (and our kitchen area certainly wasn't a standard size), but what was more special was that the colour scheme of the units was a bright yellow and white. We went over to the portacabin to look at the plans and the colouring of the kitchen tiles that the architect had specified. Yellow and white.

We had a bargain matching, fitted kitchen—from the hands of the great Designer himself.

In the middle of the second year of the work I began to think that perhaps it never would be finished. The gifts and money had come in piece by piece, as required, but the pace of work had virtually stopped.

Despite Brian's very best efforts the old lags—over 100 workers were now on his books—were getting the best out of him and they had slowed down to a snail's pace, exactly as they had wanted. The MSC had played ball too (thankfully) and extended the term of the project and increased their labour costs to cover twice the original sum. The costs of materials—our side of it—looked as if they were mounting that way too.

I decided we must take action. In January I announced that we would be moving in for the summer term, finished or not, whatever happened. This had some effect, but it wasn't until the time was up and we actually moved in that a noticeable speeding up of the work occurred.

But move in we did. We handed the old house back to the Borough and occupied the top floor of the new Charnwood centre. It was far from comfortable and the dust from the site (it was by then high summer) blew into our faces and onto our books and clothes. But the workmen got the point. Some had children of their own. They got on with the job.

A formal opening was set for 27 October 1979.

It would begin with a thanksgiving service in the nearby Methodist church and then the Mayor of Stockport would cut the ribbon. The workers now plodded on. We and the children, like voracious ants, occupied more and more of the building as work was concluded. It became a race against time, and the enthusiasm spread. It *would* be done—and it was.

October came and the church was packed with visitors and well-wishers, sponsors and supporters. We sang praises and thanks to God and then walked out into the sharp autumnal air, down St Paul's Road and over to the thin pink barrier of ribbon stretched across the front door. In addition to the Mayor, one other person was to be given the honour of cutting the ribbon and formally declaring the centre open.

Trundling up in his wheelchair to the front of the crowd came Nicholas. Nicholas, from those far-off days in the Coach House. Nicholas, whose very presence had prompted me to investigate the plight of pre-school handicapped children in Stockport. Nicholas, who, along with Nina and Felicity and so many others dearly remembered, had been the pioneers of our own first faltering efforts to care, to give something more.

The Mayor—the chief representative of the Local Authority—clasped Nicholas' weak hands in his and, hesitatingly and slowly, but with increased confidence as they grew accustomed to each other's grasp, they squeezed the scissors.

Once, twice . . . and the ribbon parted and fluttered to the ground. Wheels and feet moved forward together. It was fitting. The newly painted sign over our heads showed the new 'logo': one piece of a jigsaw, fitting into place and, underneath, the words: CHARNWOOD—For handicapped and normal children.

We had a home of our own at last.

Chapter Seventeen

OUT OF THE COLD

The afternoon has just begun. As usual the activity of the 'opportunity group' children, mothers, helpers and teachers is continual, exciting, exhausting—and not a little noisy. I am sitting on the carpeted floor with Benjamin, or perhaps Sonia. Carefully designed heating ducts ensure that warmth stays at our level.

I am attempting to encourage simple hand and eye co-ordination and I am showing the mother how to tempt the child to reach out and turn a revolving mirror. She can see her own face in the mirror and can see mummy behind. I tilt the mirror. A cloud of annoyance creeps across the intent features. Without thought, a hand pops out and the mirror is aligned again. The mother gives a surprised squeak of delight and I chime in with a loud 'Well done!' It has taken six weeks to achieve this.

I am just about to try it again when the phone rings. Janice, my secretary—whose little office doubles as 'reception' and is open to the playroom—waves at me. My problem, apparently. I get up, walk over to my office and shut the door. Janice's glance has indicated that the call should be taken privately.

'Hello, Grace Wyatt here, can I help?'

An uncertain voice greets me. 'Ooh, Mrs Wyatt?'

I re-confirm my identity. The voice at the other end, freed from the minor formality of introduction, begins to crack.

'Oh, Mrs Wyatt . . . I don't know what to do . . . I've just come from the hospital . . . They said our little David's got brain damage. What does it mean, Mrs Wyatt? They said nothing could be done . . . Oh dear—I'm so confused.'

There is the sound of sobbing at the other end of the line. I hold down hard on the sympathies of my own heart. Repetition does not make this, frequent, task any easier.

'Now, ah, sorry, what's your name, my dear?' I ask.

She gives it. Then she pleads: 'Can you help? Can you help at all? Do you know what will happen? Mother said you would. She saw you on TV. She said to call . . .'

I assure her that it is perfectly all right to call—we do have some experience of this sort of thing. Would she like to come round and see us at Charnwood?

'Could I come right now?' she asks, her voice firmer with hope. Of course she can—what better time? I tell her where to come.

An hour later a car noses slowly up the unfamiliar driveway, driven by grandmother. The caller, in her twenties, climbs out holding a not-so-little bundle. I guess, correctly, that the bundle is being held because it has not learned to walk. What are his particular problems going to be, I wonder, watching from my office. Some parents simply refuse to believe that their own child has difficulties this way. They avoid the Health Visitor and doctor until they are forced to confront the facts. Even so, it is a shock, a nasty shock, whenever handicap is confirmed.

I pop out of my office to the front porch, put on a broad smile of welcome (not difficult) and greet them. My attention is immediately on the child. The mother, I know, is badly in need of emotional support, and perhaps afraid of what she is about to see and hear.

'So this is David?' I enthuse. And well I might. He has the cheekiest little face you ever saw! Or perhaps he has the finest mop of red hair, or the very smartest outfit. Every child has something.

'Isn't he lovely! He does look a lively boy. I guess you've got your hands full with him!'

His mother, self-primed and steeled to give me the medical lowdown on his condition, is taken aback. She smiles, despite herself. She is delighted David is seen first not as a problem but as a boy. It's the first time like this she can remember, certainly from an 'expert'.

'Yes, he gets into all sorts of places—even though he can't walk yet,' she informs me.

'Really?' I say. And the child-centred conversation flows on. I offer a hand towards the front door. The conversation halts abruptly as they walk inside. They stand by Janice's desk and the varied vista of play is now open before them. They look excitedly at the happy group of twenty or so children they can see running, jumping, building, riding, talking, whispering, reading in front of them. The girl looks at me, suddenly sad, and holds David protectively closer.

'I thought you said you had handicapped children here?' she questions, anxiety creeping into her voice.

'Well, of course we do! Nearly half of those you can see have serious handicaps. Look again.'

She does, and shakes her head for a moment. Then

she notices one or two things—a hearing-aid pack here, the round features of a boy with Down's Syndrome there, a child with only one, two-fingered, hand shooting marbles across the floor.

The girl looks hard now, and I whisper in her ear, telling her what to look for. She relaxes, slowly.

'But I thought . . .' she starts.

Barbara, one of our stalwart teachers, comes up and is introduced. She runs our library of specially chosen toys, among other things. Barbara has reason to be an expert, having herself adopted four children, one seriously handicapped. She immediately excuses herself. She has promised a new mum that she would choose some good stories for her to take home and read to her little girl. Apparently she has difficulty in concentrating and the stories will help. It will also be good for her mother to see how well she can help her daughter follow them.

Barbara slips past us into an alcove on our left—the dedicated 'quiet area'. Two little girls are sitting in there, on the carpet, looking studious. Studying Paddington Bear!

I offer to show mother and daughter round. The grandmother is fascinated by all the activity going on.

'But where do you get all these helpers?' she asks. 'There are more adults here than children!'

Laughingly I agree and explain that at the afternoon opportunity group's sessions both normal and handicapped children must 'bring' their mothers. As well as the mums, there are the usual additional helpers, plus myself and the teachers. Often there are also students and other volunteers, who will be specially working with a child and his or her mother and getting to know them. This means that the mother can leave the child for a few minutes to sit down and chat to a friend, and relax from her responsibility.

I start the tour. 'This is a great favourite,' I say, and point out the sunken sandpit in the floor (though you could scarcely miss it) specially designed so that paralyzed children too can have fun in the sand, sitting or lying in it. 'And over there is the bouncing-room.' With a rubber floor, climbing-frames and trampoline, not only is this very popular with energetic boys, it is also valuable for children with movement problems.

I gesture past the cunningly trolleyed shelving and stacking toyboxes.

'In there is the kitchen—oh, yes, it's real—we do quite a lot of cooking one way and another. We made it open plan, so that the children can see what is going on.' There is a plume of steam from a kettle. A mum in jeans and jumper pours out tea for another mum, similarly dressed. Sometimes I think it is a uniform!

We move on past the kitchen alcove, and dodge instinctively as a mini shower of water jets up ahead of us.

'This,' I inform them, rather unnecessarily, 'is the water-play area. We also use it for painting and dough-making and so on.' Another jet of water shoots out, accompanied by giggles of a conspiratorial sort. What a mercy we have a tiled floor area with drain!

'Oh, there you are, Mrs Wyatt!' grins a rather embarrassed mum, turning round. 'Gemma has just learned to squirt!' Since little Gemma had barely been able to open her fingers when she arrived six months ago, I grin enthusiastically in reply.

'That is what the tiles are for,' I comment to my

amazed guests. 'Oh, and this is Wilfred.' I introduce a grave, silver-haired gentleman surrounded by eager children. 'So glad you've come.'

'It is indeed an honour,' he responds formally.

'He teaches them carpentry,' I quip. Seeing a surprised look on their faces, I add: 'Banging nails in— important skill, you see. Wilfred can coax the frailest hands to use a hammer.'

'Indubitably, Mrs Wyatt,' concurs Wilfred.

'Let's go upstairs,' I suggest.

Grandmother questions the notion. 'Upstairs? You've got stairs for handicapped children?'

'Oh, yes, we designed them deliberately. Mind you, on the plans we called them a "built-in climbing frame"! Nobody would believe we *wanted* stairs. But stairs are everywhere in normal life. The children learn to manage them beautifully with such safe ones here to practise on.'

We go upstairs and I take them into a long playroom, bounded on one side by a large, long, low mirror. One boy is making violent and absorbing faces in it, while in the corner a mother and another woman are vigorously manipulating the legs of another, smaller boy. The woman pauses and the boy's mother leans over and tries the movements herself. The boy squeaks with occasional complaint. The woman cautions the mother and shows her again.

'Our physiotherapist,' I explain, quietly, so as not to interrupt the lesson. 'But come and take a look in here.'

I lead them round through another door and we are suddenly confronted by the contorted features of the little boy in the mirror. It is one-way glass and we are now in the room at the back of it. We can see him but he cannot see us. He sees only his own reflection.

'We use this when it's important the child shouldn't know that anyone—particularly Mother—is watching. You'd be surprised what develops when no one's around!'

The sounds from the other room are loud and clear too. There are microphones in the ceiling.

We turn to the other glass panel. This looks onto yet another room—but again things are visible only from our side.

'That is the assessment room. We use it when we test the children to see how much progress they have made. Any of the mums can watch to see how her child is doing. Look, we can also watch them use it for our mini-computer,' I add. 'The children learn to use a special keyboard. It's a wonderful help—especially for deaf children and slow learners.'

We go back downstairs, mother and daughter rather overwhelmed by now, and thread our way through the busy downstairs activity towards the entrance.

'Oh, one other thing—do have a look in here. It's our toy library.' I pull open the last door, opposite Janice's desk. They both gasp. Inside is a child's paradise. All round the walls are banks of shelves—from wall to ceiling—and on them are dozens and dozens of toys. Toys for all ages and all interests. Trucks, diggers, trains and spaceships, dolls' houses, tea-sets, ponies, toys for learning, games for playing, jigsaws, jets and jack-in-the-boxes, farms, figures and fire engines. Anything you care to name. And, of course, there are many, very clever and unique toys for those with only limited skills—some individually designed by and made for us.

'Children, mums—and especially the dads (they

love it!)—can come in here and borrow two toys at a time for each child.'

'Any of these toys?' The girl is incredulous. 'But they're all brand new!'

'Oh, no, they're not actually, far from it. But we have a regular army of "experts" to make sure they stay as new as possible. Most toys can be mended and painted up again—we wouldn't buy them if they couldn't be—and we don't mind, really, if they come back dirty or broken. It shows the child has enjoyed it, used it. Toys that stay in boxes are useless.'

The mother smiles. 'It's so lovely here. It's nothing like I imagined. It's not like a school. It's more like . . .' she struggles to find the words to fit the image she has formed in her brief and quite traumatic introduction '. . . like a home.'

Two other mothers, nursing mugs of tea in the library room, nod in friendly agreement.

'Would you be able to help David if I brought him? The doctor says there is nothing that can be done. But I'm not so sure now.'

'Come across to my office and we'll talk about it,' I promise.

Outside, things have gone strangely quiet. Then, nearly as one, thirty childish voices (and several others) all strike up in time, if not in tune, with the piano.

'Happy birthday to you! Happy birthday to you! Happy birthday, dear Di-anne, happy birthday to you!'

There is a cheer and a round of applause. We go out to watch. A small mouth puckers at the head of the table and hovers dangerously close to four lighted candles on top of a cake which has been transported ceremonially from the kitchen during the official rendering of the song.

'Phew!' she blasts. One candle goes out. The others flicker but stay alight, illuminating smiling, expectant faces—both children and adults. Her two dining companions at the end of the long table try to sneak in a puff of their own but Dianne is too quick. She rocks back in her chair and there is a click of callipers against the table. 'Phew, Phew!' She does a double blast and they're out!

There is another round of clapping and cheering. Dianne glows with pride. She is multiply handi-capped, her puffing companions normal. They grin and nudge her with excitement. What is a birthday without friends?

Di, my deputy, or Irene, our nursery-aide stalwart, retrieves the cake for cutting.

It is a fairly typical Charnwood afternoon.

Chapter Eighteen

THE PHILOSOPHY OF CHARNWOOD

The 1981 Education Act was drafted to express, in legal terms, the latest ideas concerning the educational needs of handicapped children—ideas that twenty years before would have seemed fanciful and even harmful.

In the past, by concentrating on ways to meet the special needs of handicapped children, certain aspects of their development were often overlooked. It may seem trite, now, to say that most handicapped children are 'more normal than handicapped'. But it is only very recently that the *child* has been seen first, rather than the handicap.

Like all children, handicapped children need to grow up in a secure home and learn to relate gradually to the wider world of adults and other children. Unhappily the traditional assignment of a child to a special school at an early age may cut him off from his local community and also prevent him getting to know the local children who should be his natural friends.

In addition, the intensive intervention of professionals into his life—offering therapy, assessment and advice—may intrude into the normal life of the family, serving as a continual reminder of their problems.

The 1981 Education Act is an attempt to look at the real needs of the handicapped and to encourage parents to express their own ideas and wishes for their child's education. The 'we know best' philosophy has been abandoned. Parents can contribute—are expected to contribute—their intimate knowledge of their child *as a person* to add to the professional's more general experience. Parents are also asked to consider education for their child in normal school provision as both valid and possible. At Charnwood our two major themes have always been seen as 'parents as partners' and 'integrated education for both normal and handicapped children'. The 1981 Act, for us, was a legal consolidation and confirmation of so much of the work and thinking we have tried to demonstrate at Charnwood through the years.

Originally our approach sprang from a Christian viewpoint—and our direct, practical experience since then has underlined its validity.

We believe that the family group—a God-given provision for human need—is still, however poor or inadequate, the best environment in which to nurture the growing child.

Because of this we were challenged to do everything we could to enhance the parents' commitment to the child in the family context and to avoid creating divisions by interfering in the home life or undermining the parents' self-confidence in managing their own children. Their way of doing things may not always seem the best way, the most practical, the most suitable for therapy. But, as long as it is safe and (within sensible limits) effective, it is the way *for them*.

Mothers, who live intimately with their child night and day, so often do know best. They may not be able to say why. Only a small percentage are educationally or medically qualified to do so. But they know. As one paediatrician put it: 'You must listen to mothers. They not only have eyes: they have microscopes!' Parents must be partners. We should support, not supplant their efforts.

As Christians we were also convinced of the equal value of all children in God's sight and of their need to be offered the individual love and attention they deserved within our community—not relegated to some faraway institution. We have been privileged to see how many parents and children have grown together, maturing in skills and finding a comfortable place where they belong—at home.

Adjustments have been significant on all sides. And it is very important to realize that integration works both ways. For a child who is normal to be aware that others exist who are disabled is a major lesson in itself. But to go on to discover a personality in a multiply handicapped child: to make a friend, find a confidante, or meet a competitor even, is a priceless discovery. A relationship is formed. In a sense the handicap disappears: it is a limitation, per- haps, but something their friend has always had. There is certainly no fear of how to handle handicap in others—a fear that the older generation (the generation of separate development) still has.

I recall one mother telling me once the reason why she had brought her two, normal, pre-school children across Stockport to come to Charnwood, rather than take them to a local playgroup. She specially wanted them, she said, to mix with and meet handicapped children and learn from the experience. 'I often feel embarrassed when I meet someone in a wheelchair, or who is deaf. I want my children to do better,' she said.

It is true of all of us that we fear the unknown. The new, more integrated generation will, I hope, be more fearless.

Having said that, nothing in life can really prepare anyone to become the parent of a handicapped child and, when it happens, a whole range of emotions is aroused, which causes anxiety far beyond the simple problem of having to cope.

'Am I odd?'

'Am I the only one who daren't admit that I'm not sure I want this child?'

'Is it all my fault?' And so on.

Such thinking is often confused and conflicting. A parent may feel both revulsion and protection, anger and grief, bereavement and guilt. Unexpectedly, perhaps these reactions are often shared by the professionals who work with the family, and also, to a varying degree by the wider community of grandparents, neighbours—even local shopkeepers and tradesmen.

We all feel a powerful emotional response—an inbuilt sense of revulsion—when we see a handicapped person, or more particularly a child. And many are ashamed of themselves for this. I myself used to be—but more recently I have come to believe that this shows simply that we are human. We have a God-given desire for perfection, a longing for beauty and wholeness, never more evident than in our response to a new-born child. Naturally we are jolted when we see something or someone imperfect or damaged. But God has also given us the compassion to move beyond the imperfect, the handicap, and see the real person within.

Other emotions parents and the community share in these circumstances are those of anger, and that frozen anger called 'depression'. These may not be recognized for what they are, but the parents and the professionals—the doctors and nurses—feel let down, betrayed. Family 'plans' have been wrecked; professional skills are seemingly made a mockery. But by whom?

Some see in this a kind of judgement from God. Others consider the very presence of a handicapped child to be the final proof that there can be no God. Or no God who cares.

From either standpoint, resentment can grow, damaging relationships between patient and doctor, husband and wife, as painful feelings are experienced that are difficult to confess.

As a Christian I have a different view. It is that as we accept the priceless gift of real freedom of choice in life (and who does not value it?), we must also accept the possibility of unhappy results. It is no choice if the apparent options are only a 'safe game'. If we choose to marry someone who, entirely unknown to us, has a similar genetic flaw to one we happen to have, as a couple we carry a high risk of producing a handicapped child.

What would we want God to do about it? Prevent the marriage? Suddenly change our genetic make-up? When I choose to use a sharp knife—should God change the blade to rubber whenever I wield it too clumsily, so that I don't cut my finger? We could not live in such a universe—for there would be no genuine freedom at all.

Reluctantly we have to accept that, whether deliberate or not, our choices can cause us suffering and can bring pain to others. We all admit that we sometimes choose to be selfish or cruel. Should God merely leave us to get on with it, or should he interfere to prevent or punish? If he prevents our action, where is our freedom? If he punishes, where should he begin? Is anyone truly without guilt?

God in his wisdom has chosen to offer us freedom, but freedom 'within the law'—that is, within the basic guidelines he has set down for our welfare. No other freedom is real. God orders the world according to his scientific laws—we can predict the rise of the sun and the universal effect of gravity. In a similar way, God has laid down laws of justice and love, which have been there for people to understand and follow for thousands of years. Yet we are unable and unwilling to keep them. For this reason, at an exactly predicted place and time, Jesus Christ, God's Son, was born and grew up in our world, to demonstrate by his unique life and death that God hated these evil things people did, and was grieved by the suffering they caused. At the same time, however, he loved the evil-doer and wanted to offer each of us a different way to live—a means to remove the barrier wrongdoing creates between ourselves and God, to make forgiveness and a new life possible.

To achieve this, in a way we shall never fully understand, Jesus Christ took personal responsibility for our wrongdoings—our selfishness and violence—our share in the sins of the human race. He experienced God's condemnation and died 'for the sins of mankind'. His death seemed the useless end of a marvellous life. But his resurrection, witnessed by so many ordinary people, began a new era in God's dealing with you and me. Now there was a new choice. Every person could now, if they wanted, choose to start a new relationship with God—a Father-child relationship as members of his family. Not God as a kind of Father Christmas, who only wants his children to be happy, but God as a real Father who wants them to be full of love and goodness, and who has the resources available to help them achieve this.

The Christian philosopher, writer and war-time broadcaster C. S. Lewis once illustrated the possibilities that pain can offer us.

He said: 'God whispers to us in our pleasures, speaks to us in our conscience, but shouts in our pain. *It is his megaphone to rouse a deaf world.*'

In life we literally, and philosophically, 'widen or wizen'. Pain and suffering add their contribution to make us either bitter, resentful and escapist—or, after reeling under their initial onslaught, to force us to take stock and sort out what really matters. Then, if we look beyond the commonplace, we can receive what God offers and turn to share with others what he is giving of his love and comfort.

ROBERT—A POSTSCRIPT

As I was concluding the final chapters of this story of Charnwood I received the sad news that one of our 'special children', Robert, had died. The news is particularly difficult to take because Robert, though suffering from Down's Syndrome and a severe heart abnormality, has been a vivacious and outgoing little boy, who has charmed us all.

He could speak only a very little, but the varied expressions on his face and his quick hand-signals made up for this, showing us the things that interested him (and they were many) and indicating the things he particularly wanted to do.

His mother, Pat, and grandfather, 'Pop', have invariably been with him in the nursery and it became their job to interpret Robert's messages when they got too complicated for us ordinary mortals to understand! From time to time I have even accused Pat of 'making it all up'—but in the end I came to accept that he was actually 'saying' all these things.

He was, in every way, a wonderful little boy, and all of us at Charnwood, in addition to his family, and including his sisters, have valued every minute of his brief three years of life. I am so very aware, now, that no human words can replace him, or fill the empty space that his death has left. I know that it was a privilege to know him, nothing less, and that we can claim our 'sure and certain hope' that he will move through death to the new world that God has promised us.

We are given only a small idea and few words to describe what that will be like, but we are told that in that place no child will be handicapped, no relationship blighted, and that God will wipe away every tear. Until then we will try to share their sorrow, for Robert was precious, no . . . priceless, to us.

What Robert has come to mean to me, and to everyone at Charnwood, illustrates, perhaps more clearly than any philosophy or theology I can offer, what we are about, what God has called us to do and what—modest—success we have made in following his will. We can, I think, claim no credit, nor indeed look for any particular thanks for our efforts with regard to the children we meet and work with—for, in the final analysis, it is God himself who has given us the honour and privilege of working at Charnwood, and we are deeply grateful. After all, it wasn't *our* idea!